WONDERDADS

THE BEST DAD/CHILD ACTIVITIES IN THE TWIN CITIES

CONTACT WONDERDADS

WonderDads books may be purchased for educational and promotional use. For information, please email us at store@wonderdads.com.

If you are interested in partnership opportunities with WonderDads, please email us at partner@wonderdads.com.

If you are interested in selling WonderDads books and other products in your region, please email us at hiring@wonderdads.com.

For corrections, recommendations on what to include in future versions of the book, updates or any other information, please email us at info@wonderdads.com.

©2011 WonderDads, Inc.

Book Authored by Troy Thompson & the WonderDads Staff.

Cover & Layout Design by Crystal Langley. Proofread by Jarrod Graham & the WonderDads Staff.

All rights reserved. Printed in the United States of America.

No part of this publication may be reproduced or distributed in any form or by any means, or stored in a database or retrieval system, except as permitted under Sections 107 or 108 of the U.S. Copyright Act, without prior written permission of the publisher. This book is printed on acid-free paper.

Activities in this book should only be done with adult supervision. WonderDads encourages parents to not engage in any activities they feel could be harmful to their child or that their child may try to do again without an adult presence. WonderDads assumes no liability for any direct or indirect injuries that occur when using this book.

ISBN: 978-1-935153-46-7

First Printing, 2011

10 9 8 7 6 5 4 3 2 1

WONDERDADS
TWIN CITIES

Table of Contents

WELCOME TO WONDERDADS TWIN CITIES

Like so many other Dads, I love being with my kids, but struggle to find the right work/home balance. We are a part of a generation where Dads play much more of an active role with their kids, yet the professional and financial strains are greater than ever. We hope that the ideas in this book make it a little easier to be inspired to do something that makes you a hero in the eyes of your children.

This part of our children's lives goes by too fast, but the memories from a WonderDads inspired trip, event, meal, or activity last a long time (and will probably be laughed about when they grow up). So plan a Daddy day once a week, make breakfast together every Saturday morning, watch your football team every Sunday, or whatever works for you, and be amazed how long they will remember the memories and how good you will feel about yourself in the process.

Our warmest welcome to WonderDads.

Sincerely,

Jonathan Aspatore, **Founder & Dad**
Charlie (4) and Luke (3)

TOP 10 DAD/CHILD THINGS TO DO IN THE TWIN CITIES

TOP 5 DAD/CHILD RESTAURANTS

TOP 5 DAD/CHILD ACTIVITIES

TOP 5 DAD/CHILD OUTDOOR PARKS & RECREATION

TOP 5 DAD/CHILD THINGS TO DO ON A RAINY DAY

TOP 5 DAD/CHILD THINGS TO DO ON A HOT DAY

TOP 5 DAD/CHILD FULL-DAY ACTIVITIES

TOP 5 DAD/CHILD SPLURGES $$$

TOP 5 DAD/CHILD MOST MEMORABLE

THE BEST OF TWIN CITIES

THE BEST DAD/CHILD
RESTAURANTS

RESTAURANTS

ICHIBAN'S
Downtown

1333 Nicollet Ave.
Minneapolis, MN 55403
(612) 339-0540 | www.ichiban.ca/locat_minneapolis.php

Your child may not like sushi, but the sight of the fishy morsels floating by in the canal on little wooden boats may tempt them to try out the chopsticks. Fried bananas and tempura ice cream can serve as a satisfying backup plan.

JOE'S GARAGE
Downtown

1610 Harmon Pl.
Minneapolis, MN 55403
(612) 904-1630 | www.joes-garage.com

If you're hungry after checking out the sculpture garden and playing at Loring Park, head to Joe's and hangout on the patio with dramatic skyline views. Get a Martini Burger with Vodka Bleu Cheese sauce and olives for you and a non-alcoholic cheeseburger for the tyke.

KEY'S CAFÉ
Downtown

Minneapolis Downtown
114 S 9th St.
Minneapolis, MN 55402
(612) 339-6399 | www.keyscafe.com

The portions are big enough to share and breakfast is served all day. The scratch cooking and homemade desserts and pastries are a treat. Located on the ground floor of the Foshay Tower, Key's Café makes a convenient stop before or after you visit the observation deck on the top floor.

OLD SPAGHETTI FACTORY
Downtown

233 Park Ave.
Minneapolis, MN 55415
(612) 341-0949 | www.osf.com

You can load up on the carbs and there are oodles of noodles on the kids menu for your child. A creative kids program encourages your child to read and the Oreo cookie shakes are always a big hit.

THE MELTING POT
Downtown

80 S 9th St.
Minneapolis, MN 55402
(612) 338-9900 | www.meltingpot.com

Big pots of cheese and chocolate melted into a gooey liquid lava that you can dip all manner of morsels in and eat it on a stick. You could put a shoe in this stuff and make it taste delicious. And your child might think it's pretty cool, too.

AL'S BREAKFAST

Minneapolis North/
Northeast/Near North

413 14th Ave. SE
Minneapolis, MN 55414

It's only 10 feet wide but this Dinkytown (no pun intended) staple is a classic diner experience that makes a great spot for a memorable father/child experience. It's also convenient to University of Minnesota athletic events. Be prepared to do some do-si-dos as you wait and maneuver your way to a seat. But that's part of the charm.

BROADWAY PIZZA

Minneapolis North/
Northeast/Near North

2025 W River Rd.
Minneapolis, MN 55411
(612) 529-7745 | www.broadwaypizzaminneapolis.com

The original depot still has the caboose out front. The kids menu is affordable but it's always fun to share a pizza. A lunch buffet can bust your gut and the kids will love the train that runs along the bar.

CUPCAKE

Minneapolis North/
Northeast/Near North

3338 University Ave. SE
Minneapolis, MN 55414
(612) 378-4818 | www.cup-cake.com

If you want to coax a little cooperation out of your child, try dangling this place in front of them. As the name implies, it's loaded with colorful cupcakes and creative frosting designs. But they also have a variety of panini, salads and breakfast items. Get a pulled pork sandwich and let your child peruse the dessert selection while polishing off a grilled cheese.

MILDA'S CAFÉ

Minneapolis North/
Northeast/Near North

1720 Glenwood Ave.
Minneapolis, MN 55405
(612) 377-9460

You might think you're at Mom's place when you're at Milda's. The cooking is all scratch and the entrees fit like a glove on this cozy neighborhood's roots. Try the breakfast pancakes and eggs before heading into downtown or over to Theodore Wirth Park.

VESCIO'S

Minneapolis North/
Northeast/Near North

406 14th Ave. SE
Minneapolis, MN 55414
(612) 378-1747 | www.vesciosdinkytown.com

Classic Italian bistro that's been filling bellies since 1956. Family-owned and family-run, it's a homey place to slurp a little spaghetti and down some sodas. Check their daily specials and take advantage of their kids eat-free deals on Sundays.

PEPITOS

Powderhorn/Phillips
Minnehaha/Nokomis

4820 Chicago Ave.

Minneapolis, MN 55417

(612) 827-2928 | www.pepitosrestaurant.com

You can make a night of it at Pepitos. Enjoy a monster burrito and caramel flan in the urban Latino grill then slide next door and curl up in a loveseat at their colorful 1930s neighborhood cinema that showcases a variety of movies and musical acts. Don't forget the buttered popcorn.

SEA SALT EATERY

Powderhorn/Phillips
Minnehaha/Nokomis

4825 Minnehaha Ave.

Minneapolis, MN 55417

(612) 721-8990 | www.seasalteatery.wordpress.com

The popular seafood eatery with the large patio at Minnehaha Park is a must-stop when visiting the falls or taking a break from the playgrounds. Show how brave you are and slurp down some raw oysters while your child freaks in amazement. Fish, crab and plenty of po' boys can satisfy their hunger. They also serve Sebastian Joe's ice cream. Open April-October.

SEWARD CAFÉ

Powderhorn/Phillips
Minnehaha/Nokomis

2129 E Franklin Ave.

Minneapolis, MN 55404

(612) 332-1011| www.sewardcafempls.net

Turn off your cell phone (read the signs) and put away the credit card (cash or check only) and spend some time talking about Mother Earth at this organic garden. The patio is a great place to chill and people-watching can be a thrill. Local, fresh ingredients will liven up breakfast or lunch before heading over to the nearby Minneapolis Institute of Arts for more culture.

TILLIE'S BEAN

Powderhorn/Phillips
Minnehaha/Nokomis

2803 E 38th St.

Minneapolis, MN 55406

(612) 276-0100 | www.tilliesbean.com

They like their coffee at this mom and pop shop that feels like home. And so will you. Stop in for breakfast or lunch and enjoy the homey atmosphere. The kid-friendly menu includes such classics as peanut butter and pickle sandwiches.

TOWN TALK DINER

Powderhorn/Phillips
Minnehaha/Nokomis

2707 E Lake St.

Minneapolis, MN 55406

(612) 722-1312 | www.towntalkdiner.com

Cool, hip and always a scene, the Town Talk Diner will make your child's face explode in delight when they get a look at the crispy banana split. Cheese curds, bratburgers, pork candy (glazed and charred bacon on a stick) are also big hits en route to the ice cream prize at the end.

BAR ABILENE

Uptown/Lakes/Lyn–Lake
Lowery Hill/Linden Hills

1300 Lagoon Ave.
Minneapolis, MN 55408
(612) 825-2525 | www.barabilene.com

Head for lunch or an early dinner before the tequila crowd gets too ramped up and kids eat free every day. The cowboy/Mex fusion eatery is funky and fun and the guacamole is made right at the table. Very kid friendly and close to the lakes.

D'AMICO & SONS

Uptown/Lakes/Lyn–Lake
Lowery Hill/Linden Hills

2210 Hennepin Ave. S
Minneapolis, MN 55405
(612) 374-1858 | www.damicoandsons.com

The gourmet Italian dishes are always satisfying and the wood-fired pizzas are delicious. The children's menu is nicely affordable and there's plenty on it to make a hungry kid happy. Go on Sunday afternoon or evenings and kids will eat free.

DULONO'S PIZZA

Uptown/Lakes/Lyn–Lake
Lowery Hill/Linden Hills

607 W Lake St.
Minneapolis, MN 55408
(612) 827-1726

Dulono's is one of those neighborhood hole-in-the-wall joints that just throws off a good vibe. It may be a little overshadowed by some of the nearby Uptown glitz, but it's worth finding. Grab some thin-crust pizza and some cheesy bread and snarf down an old-school pizza pie complete with sodas in red plastic glasses.

FAMOUS DAVE'S

Uptown/Lakes/Lyn–Lake
Lowery Hill/Linden Hills

3001 Hennepin Ave. #G109
Minneapolis, MN 55408
(612) 822-9900 | www.famousdaves.com

This isn't like their numerous BBQ shacks and restaurants that keep growing in popularity. Their flagship Calhoun Square digs feature a unique atmosphere complete with an elevated train rumbling intermittently overhead. The BBQ is the same great stuff served elsewhere, though. Let your child's face get slathered in the sauce and take a picture for the graduation open house. They'll love it.

YUM!

Uptown/Lakes/Lyn–Lake
Lowery Hill/Linden Hills

4000 Minnetonka Blvd.
St. Louis Park, MN 55416
(612) 922-4000 | www.yumkitchen.com

Macaroni and cheese, grilled cheese sandwiches, homemade cupcakes displayed everywhere in bright colors and creatively topped...New York Strip steak with a porcini glaze or bleu cheese-crusted filet mignon. Yep. Sounds like a win-win situation for everybody involved. Aptly named and convenient to the Chain of Lakes.

RESTAURANTS

BIG DADDY'S BBQ
Como/Midway/Frogtown

625 University Ave.
St. Paul, MN 55104
(651) 222–2516 | www.bigdaddysbbq-stpaul.com

Grab some grub to go from this summertime take-out giant and plant yourself on the green grass at Como for a kingly feast. You'll be the big daddy when the tot gets a gander of the dinosaur-sized Flintstone Ribs. The hickory-smoked slabs are cooked on the outdoor grill and you can follow the hunger-inducing aroma down University Ave. to locate them.

COMO PARK PAVILLON (BLACK BEAR CROSSING)
Como/Midway/Frogtown

1360 N Lexington Pkwy
St. Paul, MN 55103
(651) 488-4920 | www.blackbearcrossings.com

Grab some fresh fruit and animal crackers at this lakeside eatery in the historic Como Park Pavilion building. The menu is refreshingly original and tasty, and the view's not bad either. Get a paddleboat just outside the door and take a quick spin around the lake and as long as you're in the neighborhood you might as well catch the Sparky the Seal show up at the zoo. It's always free.

KEY'S CAFÉ
Como/Midway/Frogtown

767 Raymond Ave
St. Paul, MN 55114
(651) 646-5756 | www.keyscafe.com

The desserts are just as good as their other locations and so is the food. Grab a bite before taking a river drive and enjoy the homemade scratch cooking and family atmosphere. Grab some pastries or cookies to go and polish them off on the bluffs high above the Mississippi.

PORKY'S DRIVE-IN
Como/Midway/Frogtown

1890 University Ave. West
St. Paul, MN 55104
(651) 644-1790

A giant pink pig in a top hat greets you as you pull in. Pork out on the burgers that come with a crispy-fried onion ring smashed into the top of the bun while you sit in the car. Classic cars are a common sight and hearken back to the days before clowns and kings.

SNUFFY'S MALT SHOP
Como/Midway/Frogtown

1125 Larpenteur Ave. W
St. Paul, MN 55113
(651) 488-0241 | www.snuffysmaltshop.com
Treat the tyke to a classic American experience and grab a burger and fries in this Happy Days throwback. Thick blended malts come with the tin to ensure you don't miss a drop. Decadent sundaes, floats, fudge brownies and Snuffy Coladas are other tempting options.

BON VIE CAFÉ/
Highland/Grove-Macaliter/ Summit Hill

A PIECE OF CAKE BAKERY

518 Selby Ave.
St. Paul, MN 55102
(651) 287-0112 | www.apieceofcakebakery.net
The bright and sunny Bon Vie is a good spot to people–watch through the large front windows. The food is fresh and the menu changes frequently. Enjoy a good meal and an espresso over the funny papers then stroll up the block to their sister property, A Piece of Cake. It's an entire shop filled to the rafters with cake and frosting. Oh, there are plenty of muffins, cookies, bars and pastries, too.

CHATTERBOX PUB
Highland/Grove-Macaliter/ Summit Hill

800 Cleveland Ave. South
St. Paul, MN 55116
(651) 699-1154 | www.chatterboxpub.net
Face off over a table-top game of Battleship or teach your child the finer points of Donkey Kong and Space Invaders on the Atari while you wait for your food at this hip neighborhood bar and grill. You'll enjoy the gourmet burgers and sandwiches while your child can sip on a house-made brew of Cheshire Cat root beer along with their kids' meal. Cookies included.

GRAND OLE CREAMERY
Highland/Grove-Macaliter/ Summit Hill

750 Grand Ave.
St. Paul, MN 55105
(651) 293-1655 | www.grandolecreamery.com
The pizza is pretty good. Really good, actually, considering this is an ice cream parlor. And what an ice cream parlor it is. After noshing on the Italian pie, check out the scads of thick and creamy flavor concoctions. It will take a little time to decide what to put on top of your homemade waffle cone, but it's a solid investment for the payback.

19

GROVELAND TAP

Highland/Grove-Macaliter/
Summit Hill

1834 St. Clair Ave.
St. Paul, MN 55105
(651) 699-5058 | www.grovelandtap.com

It's the kind of man-cave you wish was in your basement, but with a kids' menu. This popular neighborhood haunt as all the basics, but for real adventure introduce your child to their version of the famous Juicy Lucy—a hearty burger with a molten cheese-lava core. It's hot, so be careful. Play some vids in the game room and jam the jukebox for a bit while you bond.

PUNCH PIZZA

Highland/Grove-Macaliter/
Summit Hill

704 Cleveland Ave. S
St. Paul, MN, 55116
(651) 696-1066 | www.punchpizza.com

Fantastic pizza anytime, but on cold winter days it's an especially nice place to warm up after sledding the hills at Highland Park. The large wood-fired brick oven will help take the chill out as well as make the traditional Neapolitan pizza taste great. There's plenty of apple juice to help wash it down and the river is just out the door to explore during warm-weather trips.

AXEL'S BONFIRE GRILL

Phalen/Dayton's Bluff/
Woodbury

1424 Weir Dr.
Woodbury, MN 55125
(651) 735-0085 | www.axelsbonfire.com

It's classy and casual and always consistent. The wood-fired grill makes for a cozy atmosphere and you can enjoy a high-quality meal and let your child create and build their own pizza. When your little chef finishes that, they can make their own sundae for dessert.

MAGNOLIA'S

Phalen/Dayton's Bluff/
Woodbury

1081 Payne Ave.
St. Paul, MN 55130
(651) 774-3333 | www.magnolia-stpaul.com

A classic Minnesota café tucked away in a friendly neighborhood setting, Magnolia's has plenty to satisfy. From the quintessential Friday night fish fries to breakfast and burgers, Magnolia's cooks it right. The kids will love the fried chicken and caramel apple pie a la mode.

MAMA'S PIZZA

Phalen/Dayton's Bluff/
Woodbury

961 Rice St.
St. Paul, MN 55117
(651) 489-2005 | www.mamaspizzaparlor.com

You can almost envision a couple of animated dogs slurping up noodles together here, red and white checkered tablecloths and all. The spaghetti and meatballs are tasty and the pizza pies are even better. They even come heart-shaped on Valentine's. Finish the night on the couch watching Lady and the Tramp.

SWEDE HOLLOW CAFÉ

Phalen/Dayton's Bluff/
Woodbury

725 7th St. E
St. Paul, MN 55106
(651) 776-8810 | www.swedehollowcafe.com

All those stairs down to the ravine at Swede Hollow Park across the street are going to require some extra energy, and this is the place to get zapped. They serve artisan espresso, lingonberry waffles and caramel rolls as well as a variety of sandwiches and baked goods. The kids love hanging out in their garden on the patio and a trip down to the natural playground of the Hollow will work off any extra calories.

YARUSSO-BROS.

Phalen/Dayton's Bluff/
Woodbury

637 Payne Ave.
St. Paul, MN 55130
(651) 776-4848 | www.yarussos.com

Feel free to sneeze; it won't budge these meatballs from the top of the spaghetti. The kids can eat for free at their Sunday brunch, but the prices aren't going to break your wallet during the rest of the week. It's a neighborhood institution with noodles and cheese galore...and really big meatballs.

BLACK DOG

St. Paul Downtown

308 Prince St.
St. Paul, MN 55101
(651) 228-9274 | www.blackdogstpaul.com

If all the fresh foods and activities at the farmer's market in Lowertown are making you hungry, then slip into the Black Dog just across the street. There's lots of eye candy on the walls and the artsy interior has a cool, beatnik vibe. Don't be surprised if the echoes of bongos are still bouncing around from the night before. There's plenty to satisfy younger taste buds and your sophisticated palate won't complain either.

COSETTA'S

St. Paul Downtown

211 7th St. W
St. Paul, MN 55102
(651) 222-3476

It's a great stop if you're going to the Excel Energy Center for a Wild game or any other event. Even if you live on Mars, it's worth the drive. Pick the pizza line (there's another one for sandwiches) and pick up some out of this world cafeteria-style pizza. They have plenty of chocolate milk on hand, too.

MANCINI'S

St. Paul Downtown

531 7th St. W
St. Paul, MN 55102
(651) 224-7345 | www.mancinis.com

Enjoy a timeless supper club experience at this Rat Pack-chic steakhouse that is as entertaining for its endless character as it is for its food. Buses and trolleys travel to Wild, Twins and Viking games as well as other events. Use this classic family-run eatery as your headquarters to enjoy an outing, then get some lobster (go ahead and splurge) and chargrilled steaks in the dining room. Try not to fill up on the garlic bread.

MICKEY'S DINER

St. Paul Downtown

36 7th St. W
St. Paul, MN 55102
(651) 222-5633 | www.mickeysdiningcar.com

Drop a quarter in the slot of one of the table-top jukeboxes and order up some classic dining car grub. The iconic flashing lights on the outside aren't nearly as electric as scoring a seat at the counter and watching the mounds of hash browns fly all over the flat-top right in front of you. The waitresses will take good care of you and aren't bashful about publicly, and humorously, scolding you if you misbehave. Perfect for any downtown excursion.

RED'S SAVOY PIZZA

St. Paul Downtown

421 7th St. E
St. Paul MN 55101
(651) 227-1437

It's all about the pizza at Red's. Pretend you're going to a pizza cave on a bright sunny day and your child will believe it actually is one once you enter the windowless confines. But the legendary pies come loaded with enough bubbly mozzarella to shine a happy cheesy light onto any size kid's face. Even big ones like you.

BOCA CHICA

West Side/South St. Paul/
Inver Grove Heights/
Eagan/Mendota Heights

11 Cesar Chavez St.
St. Paul, MN 55107
(651) 222-8499 | www.bocachicarestaurant.com

Just a couple of hops from the Wabasha Street Caves, Boca Chica's lunch buffet is an all-you-can-eat fiesta. The atmosphere is pure Mexico and the intriguing murals that dominate the walls mirror the large colorful artwork that is painted on the sides of many neighborhood buildings. The District del Sol area is rich in culture with endless cheese enchiladas and tacos.

BUCCA DI BEPPO'S

West Side/South St. Paul/
Inver Grove Heights/
Eagan/Mendota Heights

2728 Gannon Rd.
St. Paul, MN 55116
(651) 772-4388 | www.bucadibeppo.com

The portions are extreme and most are served family-style so you can share and work on your "please pass the cheesy bread Florentine" skills. There's a colossal brownie sundae for dessert that could feed a large family if you want to go over the top and get a good "Wow!" Don't forget to ask for one of those nifty plastic pocket protectors to take home.

CHUCK E. CHEESE'S

West Side/South St. Paul/
Inver Grove Heights/
Eagan/Mendota Heights

1422 Robert St. S
West St. Paul, MN 55118
(651) 453-1066 | www.chuckecheese.com

Animatronic animals entertain you with song while you eat (new show every few minutes) and you could spend hours afterward whacking moles or firing tokens into dragon mouths. The carnival-type atmosphere is always a hit with kids and there is plenty of space and play area to run wild in addition to the bonanza of arcade games.

EL BURRITO MERCADO

West Side/South St. Paul/
Inver Grove Heights/
Eagan/Mendota Heights

175 Cesar Chavez St.
St. Paul, MN 55107
(651) 227-2192 | www.elburritomercado.com

The cafeteria-style restaurant in the back of this grocery store hybrid is a unique destination that serves a smorgasbord of Mexican delights. You can get some fresh-roasted Mexican corn on a stick in the parking lot out back or enjoy the outdoor patio and taco grill. Playground equipment is just across the street and there might be some ethnic dance or musical performances going on in the plaza next door. Be prepared to leave with one of the colorful piñatas that dangle throughout the aisles.

RESTAURANTS

RIVERBOAT GRILL

West Side/South St. Paul/
Inver Grove Heights/
Eagan/Mendota Heights

105 Harriet Island Rd.
St. Paul, MN 55107
(651) 290-2363 | www.riverboatgrill.com

Play on the steamboat-shaped playground at Harriet Island Park, then walk over to the docks and grab a seat on the roof of a real riverboat for some cheese curds or French fries. The downtown St. Paul skyline towers over the river from the bluff-tops across the water and if you're lucky you can get an up–close view of a mammoth barge as it attempts to navigate the bridges. Don't be surprised if you're joined by a few ducks. Open seasonally.

IKEA

Bloomington/Eden Prairie/
Richfield/Edina

8000 Ikea Way
Minneapolis, MN 55425
(952) 858-8088 | www.ikea.com

The restaurant inside the stadium-sized home and furnishing store is one of the best deals around. You can pick up a stylish entertainment center for the new flat-screen and enjoy some dirt-cheap Swedish meatballs and lingonberry soda all in one stop. It's extremely kid friendly, extremely busy, and totally Minnesota.

LION'S TAP

Bloomington/Eden Prairie/
Richfield/Edina

16180 Flying Cloud Dr.
Eden Prairie, MN 55347
(952) 934-5299 | www.lionstap.com

Juicy hamburgers that squirt and dribble all over your chin and a chilled mug of heady root beer drawn from a tap handle. Mmmm. Hanging out with your buddy is easy in this place. There are plenty of screens to catch the game on, too.

MALL OF AMERICA FOOD COURTS

Bloomington/Eden Prairie/
Richfield/Edina

60 East Broadway
Bloomington, MN 55425
(952) 883-8800 | www.mallofamerica.com

If you can't find something to please even the most finicky of eaters at one of the food courts overlooking the mega-mall amusement park, then professional intervention might be required. The bigger problem might be in sitting still long enough to swallow with all of the roller coasters, Ferris wheels and other rides beckoning below.

Q CUMBERS

Bloomington/Eden Prairie/
Richfield/Edina

7465 France Ave. S
Edina, MN 55435
(952) 831-0235 | www.qcumbers.com

Kids can eat on Monday nights for a buck and you don't have to feel guilty about it. There's a 50-foot salad bar and a wide variety of hot entrees and other goodies on the well-stocked buffet. Many of the items are made with seasonally-fresh local organic ingredients.

RAINFOREST CAFÉ

Bloomington/Eden Prairie/
Richfield/Edina

102 South Ave.
Bloomington, MN 55425
(952) 854-7500 | www.rainforestcafe.com

Take a trek to the jungle and enjoy the wild atmosphere of the Rainforest Café. There are plenty of critter characters to entertain from the surrounding canopy of greenery and the thundering rainstorms that constantly threaten will excite the kids to finish before the downpour starts. Of course, you know better.

DONATELLI'S

Roseville/White Bear Lake/
Shoreview/Blaine

2692 E County Rd. E
White Bear Lake, MN 55110
(651) 777-9199 | www.donatellis.com

Your hearty Italian meal will probably be big enough to satisfy both of you and there's always the delicious pizza to consider as well. The décor is just as charmingly cheesy as anything that arrives on the plate and will keep your child thoroughly entertained.

KOZLAK'S ROYAL OAK

Roseville/White Bear Lake/
Shoreview/Blaine

4785 Hodgson Rd.
Shoreview, MN 55126
(651) 484-8484 | www.kozlaks.com

For a classy experience, head to Kozlak's for your fill of prime rib with all the trimmings. The jazz brunch on Sundays is swank and it's a great date-night option anytime. Sure, it's a little upscale, but any place that has Barney Burgers and Snoopy Sundaes on the menu can't be too stuffy.

MAPLEWOOD MALL FOOD COURT

Roseville/White Bear Lake/
Shoreview/Blaine

3001 White Bear Ave. N
Maplewood, MN 55109
(651) 770-5020 | www.simon.com

There are plenty of options available for chow and a soft play area to help your child burn up any extra fuel. And if you need to pick up a few items for yourself, you're in luck. You've got a whole mall at your disposal.

25

GREEN MILL

Roseville/White Bear Lake/
Shoreview/Blaine

1000 Gramsie Rd.
Shoreview, MN 55126
(651) 482-1600 | www.greenmill.com

Kids can eat free on Tuesday nights and they can also help make their own pizza. They even have a smiley face pizza to provide a little extra fun. You can choose from a wide variety of sandwiches, pastas, wings and burgers.

SPACE ALIENS BAR & GRILLE

Roseville/White Bear Lake/
Shoreview/Blaine

11166 County Road 37 NE
Albertville, MN 55301
(763) 497-6718 | www.spacealiens.com

Take a ride on the mother ship and blast off into a cosmic and quirky space. The interior galaxy is full of arcades and amusements and you can choose from wood-fired pizza or BBQ-style grub. Make some tinfoil hats to wear on the drive up, but you might want to consider leaving them in the car when you get there.

A&W

Shakopee/Apple Valley/
Burnsville/Lakeville

7641 150th St. W
Apple Valley, MN 55124
(952) 431-5414 | www.awrestaurants.com

Root beer floats are the star at this classic American burger stop. Eat from the car window and order through the speakers for the total experience. It's been around longer than the flashy newcomers so you also get a little bit of nostalgia from your youth.

BUCCA DI BEPPO

Shakopee/Apple Valley/
Burnsville/Lakeville

14300 Burnhaven Dr.
Burnsville, MN 55306
(952) 892-7272 | www.buccadibeppo.com

A trip to the bathroom is thoroughly entertaining and there's kitschy and cheeky material splattered over every inch of wall space to keep you both entertained. Dine on family-style dishes to a heavy dose of Dean Martin and try to nab the table in the kitchen for a truly unique experience.

CHAMPP'S

Shakopee/Apple Valley/
Burnsville/Lakeville

1200 County Rd. 42 W
Burnsville, MN 55337
(952) 898-5050 | www.champps.com

Catch all the game action at this kid-friendly quintessential sports bar. There's a dizzying array of screens to monitor every game and the Little Champps menu has all the favorites and then some. Wear your favorite jerseys and cheer on the team with high-fives.

RAISING CANE'S

Shakopee/Apple Valley/
Burnsville/Lakeville

7501 150th St. W
Apple Valley, MN 55124
(952) 432-8700 | www.raisingcanes.com

Nearly every kid on the planet would probably rank chicken nuggets near the top of their favorite food list if such a poll were possible. You won't have to worry about a mutiny from yours if you grab a batch of these addictive little morsels.

TERESA'S

Shakopee/Apple Valley/
Burnsville/Lakeville

20202 Heritage Dr.
Lakeville, MN 55044
(952) 469-8903 | www.teresasmexicanrest.com

Pop into this popular local Mexican restaurant after a day at Lake Marion and enjoy authentic cuisine in a fun and family-friendly atmosphere. The meals come quick and the portions are plenty large.

BENIHANA

St. Louis Park/Golden Valley
Minnetonka/Maple Grove

11840 Fountains Way
Brooklyn Park, MN 55369
(763) 315-0090 | www.benihana.com

Chefs prepare the food at your table with knives twirling in a frenzy and food particles flying everywhere. If that's not enough to entertain, there's always the ceramic Buddha glass where you can stick a straw in the belly. The kids menu features smaller portions of favorites but doesn't skimp on the show.

GALAXY DRIVE-IN

St. Louis Park/Golden Valley
Minnetonka/Maple Grove

3712 Quebec Ave. S
Minneapolis, MN 55426
(952) 277-7777 | www.galaxy.drivein.com

If you can't find a place for the car, there are picnic tables on the lawn. The futuristic drive-in is eye-catching and retro at the same time. There's always plenty of activity by the lake in the summertime and the prices are impressively retro as well. Bring the pet. Open seasonally.

MINNETONKA DRIVE-IN

St. Louis Park/Golden Valley
Minnetonka/Maple Grove

4658 Shoreline Dr.
Spring Park, MN 55384
(952) 471-9383

It's in a great location to enjoy the lake with nearby beaches, fishing and boating options. The hot rods come cruising in droves on Thursdays and can be spotted with frequency during the rest of the week. Open seasonally.

27

PAPA'S CAFÉ

St. Louis Park/Golden Valley
Minnetonka/Maple Grove

7181 42nd Ave. N
New Hope, MN 55427
(763) 535-4887

Belly up to the counter and count the dings on the order-up bell. Papa's will help make you a big Papa with their happy diner entrees and homemade pies. It's a simple, good, fun and very reasonably priced adventure with a small neighborhood feel.

PARK TAVERN

St. Louis Park/Golden Valley
Minnetonka/Maple Grove

3401 Louisiana Ave. S
St. Louis, Park, MN 55426
(952) 929-6810 | www.parktavern.net

Challenge your child to a few games of bowling at this popular entertainment complex that serves good food cheap. There are plenty of amusements and activities to keep you occupied between games. It's not a fair contest if you use the gutter rails, too, so play nice.

THE BEST DAD/CHILD
ACTIVITIES

MILL CITY MUSEUM

Downtown

704 S 2nd St.
Minneapolis, MN 55401
(612) 341-7555 | www.millcitymuseum.org

Who knew flour could be so much fun? Built in the ruins of an old flour mill that used St. Anthony Falls for power, the museum has plenty of history about Minneapolis' infancy and hands-on activities for kids. Hop in the flour tower elevator for a fun ride.

MINNEAPOLIS CENTRAL LIBRARY

Downtown

300 Nicollet Mall
Minneapolis, MN 55401
(952) 847-8000 | www.hclib.org

Curl up in one of the many quiet nooks of the bright and airy Minneapolis library system crown jewel. There are five floors of books to explore and plenty of high-tech bells and whistles to help you navigate.

MINNEAPOLIS FARMERS MARKET

Downtown

312 E Lyndale Ave.
Minneapolis, MN 55405
(612) 333-1718 | www.mplsfarmersmarket.com
Open seasonally

Head to one of the largest open-air markets in the Midwest and stock up on some of the freshest locally sourced ingredients around. You'll find everything you need among the rows of colorful displays to create a special meal together as well as a few treats to tide you over.

MINNEAPOLIS QUEEN

Downtown

Boom Island
(952) 474-8058 | www.twincitiescruises.com
Mother's Day – October

Let your inner-Tom Sawyer out and explore the Mississippi aboard a classic 78-foot paddlewheel boat. Snacks and beverages are on board and you'll get an up-close experience of the lock and dam.

SUMMER MUSIC & MOVIES

Downtown

Boom Island
www.mplsmusicandmovies.com

Frisbees, flip-flops and food are side attractions at the popular summer series in Loring Park that combines free outdoor concerts and twilight movies on the big screen. Go see the spoon and cherry or giant glass fish in the sculpture garden across the bridge before the show. Don't forget the lawn chairs or blankets.

ROLLERDOME AT THE METRODOME

Downtown

November-March
www.roller-dome.com

When the lakes are frozen and there's too much snow on their surrounding paths, lace up the Rollerblades and zoom around the concrete concourses of the Metrodome. The facility opens for use on a varying schedule during the winter months and attracts quite the crowd to the two-level track.

MINNESOTA ORCHESTRA

Downtown

1111 Nicollet Ave.
Minneapolis, MN 55403
(612) 371-5600 | www.minnesotaorchestra.com

The Minnesota Orchestra has been known to rock a little Amadeus in their time and their free outdoor summer concert series is a great way to expose your potential prodigy to classical music. Fun and informal, the events are always well-attended and a young people's concert series can let you experience the majesty of the Orchestra Hall interior for about the cost of a drive-thru meal.

ARTICULTURE

Minneapolis North/
Northeast/Near North

2613 E Franklin Ave.
Minneapolis, MN 55406
(612) 729-5151 | www.articulture.org

Put on a smock and get messy with paint, clay and other art materials at this non profit community art center. There's a full schedule of classes and other events for tots as young as 1. Even if the vase comes out a little crooked, it will be a cherished keepsake.

FIREFIGHTER HALL & MUSEUM

Minneapolis North/
Northeast/Near North

664 22nd Ave. NE
Minneapolis, MN 55418
(612) 623-3817 | www.firehallmuseum.org
Saturdays: April-October

See how the heroes operate and give your child the thrill of sliding down the fire pole before hopping in one of those bright, shiny red trucks for a quick ride through the streets of the city. You'll come away being a hero, too.

JIM LUPIENT WATER PARK

Minneapolis North/
Northeast/Near North

1520 Johnson St. NE
Minneapolis, MN 55413
(612) 370-3989 | www.minneapolisparks.org

You don't have to venture out into the country to experience the fun of swimming in a rock quarry. The faux quarry at this water park is filled with foam rocks and logs to play on. And there are plenty of slippery slides and splash areas that you won't find in the boonies.

STONE ARCH BRIDGE

Minneapolis North/
Northeast/Near North

6th Ave. SE at the Mississippi River
Minneapolis, MN 55401

Pack a lunch and take a bike ride or stroll across one of Minneapolis' signature icons. The view of St. Anthony Falls and the downtown skyline is astounding and it's a great spot to appreciate the small things. You can bike for miles on the greenway, but you'll want to stop and smell the roses while on the bridge.

TEXTILE CENTER

Minneapolis North/
Northeast/Near North

3000 University Ave. SE # 100
Minneapolis, MN 55414
(612) 436-0464 | www.textilecentermn.org

Most every kid likes arts and craft time in school and the Textile Center let's your child experience creating some crafts with all manner of fibers and textiles. Check out the class schedule and explore the shop and gallery.

DAVE'S POPCORN

Powderhorn/Phillips/
Minnehaha/Nokomis

1848 E 38th St.
Minneapolis, MN 55407
(612) 743-6316 | www.davespopcorn.com
Open seasonally

There's no need to wait for the fair when Dave's Popcorn opens each spring through fall. The carnival-type popcorn stand is festively flashy and loaded with crunchy caramel corn and other goodies. It's a neighborhood tradition.

HEART OF THE BEAST PUPPET THEATER

Powderhorn/Phillips/
Minnehaha/Nokomis

1500 E Lake St.
Minneapolis, MN 55407
(612) 721-2535 | www.hobt.org

Forget the Saturday morning cartoons at home and check out the puppet shows at Heart of the Beast Theater instead. It's way more entertaining. The shows are free but there is a suggested donation. Family puppet workshops after the shows let you try your hands at being a puppeteer and you can even make your own puppet to take home.

MIDTOWN GLOBAL MARKET

Powderhorn/Phillips/
Minnehaha/Nokomis

920 E Lake St.
Minneapolis, MN 55407
(612) 872-4041 | www.midtownglobalmarket.org

Take a trip around the world and experience a staggering diversity of goods and food. There's a new surprise at every turn. Kids love the large play areas and will be entertained by performers of all sorts. The aromas from authentic ethnic restaurants mingle together with a delicious dance and jewelry, crafts and other wares are available from more than 50 vendors.

MINNEAPOLIS INSTITUTE OF ARTS

Powderhorn/Phillips/
Minnehaha/Nokomis

2400 3rd Ave. S
Minneapolis, MN 55404
(612) 870-3180 | www.artsmia.org

Enjoy a grown-up museum filled with a nationally renowned collection of artwork. The stately exhibit halls allow for extensive roaming. A kid's activity center is loaded with games and crafts and their monthly family days put performers and artists into the mix. Best of all, it's all free, though donations are accepted.

BAKKEN MUSEUM

Minneapolis Uptown /Lakes/
Lyn–Lake/Lowry Hill/Linden Hills

3537 Zenith Ave. S
Minneapolis, MN 55416
(612) 926-3878 | www.thebakken.org

Watch Frankenstein come to life in this quirky museum about medical electricity and magnets. Hands-on experiments can zap some life into any afternoon and it is conveniently located near the shores of Lake Calhoun for plenty of outdoor adventure.

COMO-HARRIET STREETCAR

Minneapolis Uptown /Lakes/
Lyn–Lake/Lowry Hill/Linden Hills

www.trolleyride.org

Hop aboard a trolley and cruise the streets of the city in a blast from the past. The nostalgic yellow train cars ride the rails during seasonal operation and a museum at the depot houses a variety of other trolleys from Minneapolis' transportation past.

INTERMEDIA ARTS

Minneapolis Uptown /Lakes/
Lyn–Lake/Lowry Hill/Linden Hills

2822 S Lyndale Ave.
Minneapolis, MN 55408
(612) 871-4444 | www.intermediaarts.org

Let your child get their creative juices flowing at this multi-discipline educational center for the arts. Classrooms and workshops, many free, will let you explore video game creation, writing, performance art and even hip-hop beats and rhymes.

LEONARDO'S BASEMENT

Minneapolis Uptown /Lakes/
Lyn–Lake/Lowry Hill/Linden Hills

4301 Nicollet Ave. S
Minneapolis, MN 55409
(612) 824-4394 | www.leonardosbasement.org

You can help make hands-on creations at this outfit's facilities in the art-rich lakes area. Saturday open sessions allow for the exploration of a variety of projects and regular activities such as LEGO leagues and robotic groups provide potential for bringing a plastic Godzilla to life.

MUSIC & MOVIES IN THE PARK

Minneapolis Uptown /Lakes/
Lyn–Lake/Lowry Hill/Linden Hills

4135 W Lake Harriet Pkwy.
Minneapolis, MN 55410
(612) 370-4856 | www.minneapolisparks.org

The Lake Harriet band shell is the gravitational center of the lakes area's summer evenings. A full slate of lakeside concerts, movies and other events make for cool evenings no matter what the temperature.

SEBASTIAN JOE'S

Minneapolis Uptown /Lakes/
Lyn–Lake/Lowry Hill/Linden Hills

2822 S Lyndale Ave.
4321 Upton Ave. South
Minneapolis, MN 55410
(612) 926-7916 | www.sebastianjoesicecream.com

It's just a short stroll from the lake and worth a trip from anywhere. Delicious homemade ice cream served in a fresh waffle cone, dipped in chocolate and sprinkled with colorful nuggets is a sight to behold and you'll both enjoy the variety of flavors and other offerings this city favorite offers.

A PRAIRIE HOME COMPANION

St. Paul Downtown

www.prairiehome.publicradio.com

See all the Lake Wobegon characters in action as they do their live weekly radio broadcast from the historic Fitzgerald Theater in downtown. A variety of musical acts, comedy skits and storytelling fill the evening and is a Minnesota original. Check the calendar for seasonal performance schedules.

CANDYLAND

St. Paul Downtown

435 Wabasha St. N
St. Paul, MN 55102
(612) 292-1191 | www.candylandstore.com

Watch your child burst into the Snoopy happy dance the moment you step in to this tiny wonderland filled with fresh candies of all sorts. Marvel at the colors behind the enormous glass display cases and grab a sack of sugar before you visit the Science Museum or Children's Museum. If you're lucky, you can even watch them make the next batch of treats.

MINNESOTA CHILDREN'S MUSEUM

St. Paul Downtown

10 7th St. W
St. Paul, MN 55102
(651) 225-6000 | www.mcm.org

Join in the play activities and hands-on exhibits that will have you discovering dinosaurs and building snow castles indoors. Five permanent exhibit rooms and rotating feature exhibits provide ample opportunities to get involved. Tuesdays are kept group-free and special free days are scheduled monthly.

MINNESOTA HISTORY CENTER

St. Paul Downtown

345 Kellogg Blvd. W
St. Paul, MN 55102
(651) 259-3000 | www.minnesotahistorycenter.org

History is far from a snooze-inducing subject at the Minnesota History Center. Join your child in a re–created farm house basement as a mock tornado passes overhead and jam out to the homegrown sounds of Bob Dylan and Prince in an interactive experience geared for young and old alike.

OMNI THEATER

St. Paul Downtown

120 Kellogg Blvd. W
St. Paul, MN 55102
(651) 221-9444 | www.smm.org

Sit back and stare at the ceiling in this giant domed theater that projects a rotating menu of wonders overhead. The hi-tech inner-workings are on display in the lobby and the process provides a totally immersive experience no matter what the show.

SCIENCE MUSEUM OF MINNESOTA

St. Paul Downtown

120 Kellogg Blvd. W
St. Paul, MN 55102
(651) 221-9444 | www.smm.org

Get sneezed on, explore mystery smells (good and bad) and work the giant T–Rex jaws. Endless opportunities abound to get in on the action in this touchy-feely science experiment bonanza. A rooftop tugboat seems out of place high above the river below and the backyard putt-putt course explores the different regions of the state complete with trademark lake and river water hazards. Don't forget to see the mummy.

ST. PAUL WINTER CARNIVAL

St. Paul Downtown

www.winter-carnival.com

There are parades, ice sculptures, outdoor concerts, games, and those pesky Vulcans that constantly roam around on their fire truck leaving marks on your face. Embrace the cold and go on a treasure hunt for the elusive medallion. Bring plenty of hot chocolate and it will feel like a day at the beach. Well...almost.

COMO ZOO

Como/Midway/Frogtown

1225 Estabrook Dr.
St. Paul, MN 55103
(651) 487-8229 | www.comozooconservatory.org

Feeding the vocally demanding sea lions out of a paper cup filled with fish heads is an experience every child should get to enjoy at least once. And Sparky the Seal has been bouncing his ball for generations. The classic inner-city zoo experience comes complete with all the requisite animals as well as a tiny-tot amusement park and indoor garden paradise.

COMO PLANETARIUM
Como/Midway/Frogtown

780 Wheelock Pkwy. W
St. Paul, MN 55117
(612) 293-5398 | www.planetarium.spps.org

Telescopes are cool. There's a whole universe out there and a visit to the planetarium can let you explore distant planets and constellations. Public shows are scheduled monthly and a drop-by visit anytime may just get you a lucky private peek of the heavens if the astronomer has the time.

GIBBS FARM MUSEUM
Como/Midway/Frogtown

2097 Larpenteur Ave. W
St. Paul, MN 55113
(651) 646-8629 | www.rchs.com

See the horse-drawn plows and watch costumed characters churn the butter at this farmhouse and barn in the middle of the city. The farm recreates life on the Minnesota prairies in the pioneering days explores Dakota Indian culture.

MINNESOTA STATE FAIR
Como/Midway/Frogtown

1265 Snelling Ave. N
St. Paul, MN 55108
(651) 288-4400 | www.mnstatefair.org

It's too big to possibly see it all in one day, so go often and experience everything the annual summer-ending bash has to offer. If the rides, carnival games, one-of-a-kind exhibits and grandstand shows aren't enough, you can always gorge on the smorgasbord of everything on a stick.

RAPTOR CENTER
Como/Midway/Frogtown

1920 Fitch Ave.
St. Paul, MN 55108
(612) 624-4745 | www.raptor.cvm.umn.edu

Weekend adventure can be had on Saturdays and Sundays at the University of Minnesota's Raptor Center. Get up close to hawks, bald eagles, and other birds with the afternoon educational programs. Keep with the animal theme and zip over to the zoo for some four-footed and finned critters.

TWIN CITY MODEL RAILROAD MUSEUM

Como/Midway/Frogtown

1021 Bandana Blvd. E
St. Paul, Minnesota 55108
(651) 647-9628 | www.tcmrm.org

Tucked in the corner of the Bandana Square depot complex is a magical fantasy world of the Twin City landscape. A giant model railroad exhibit will blow away any basement track you've seen and you can watch the choo-choos cruise around a whimsical recreation of the cities complete with miniature White Castles, street scenes and plenty of lights and whistles. Evening visits are awash in a surreal glow.

CIRCUS JUVENTAS

Highland/
Groveland-Macalaster/
Summit Hill

1270 Montreal Ave.
St. Paul, MN 55116
(651) 699-8229 | www.circusjuventas.com

Attend one of the seasonal performances of this 600-kid strong circus arts school or get involved and become part of the show. Jugglers, acrobats and balancing specialists twirl, whirl and bounce at every turn. And of course, there are plenty of clowns.

HIGHLAND PARK AQUATIC CENTER

Highland/
Groveland-Macalaster/
Summit Hill

1840 Edgcumbe Rd.
St. Paul, MN 55116
(651) 695-3773 | www.stpaul.gov

The rock climbing wall in the diving area is a big hit, as are the splash pads, slides and sprinklers. A lap pool is reserved for serious swimming, but with so many water toys around to play with this trip is better done in silly mode.

IZZY'S ICE CREAM

Highland/
Groveland-Macalaster/
Summit Hill

2034 Marshall Ave.
St. Paul, MN 55104
(651) 603-1458 | www.izzysicecream.com

For an affordable frozen treat, head to Izzy's on Marshall and try to choose from their 32 varieties of hand-crafted gourmet ice cream flavors. Grab a couple of scoops and head a few blocks west and explore the river bluffs above the Ford Dam.

JAMES J. HILL HOUSE

Highland/
Groveland-Macalaster/
Summit Hill

240 Summit Ave.
St. Paul, MN 55102
(651) 297-2555 | www.mnhs.org

The mansions on Summit Ave. make for an entertaining drive, but the granddaddy of them all is the red sandstone beast at the end. Tours are given regularly and special story time tours are geared for younger visitors. View the ornate chandeliers, art gallery and giant greenhouse and see how one of the local founding fathers lived.

HIGHLAND THEATER

Highland/
Groveland-Macalaster/
Summit Hill

760 Cleveland Ave. S
St. Paul, MN 55116
(651) 698-3035 | www.mannstheatresmn.com

Eschew the multiplex crowds and take in a show at a neighborhood theater with classic marquis glitz. Sure, the seats are hard and the digital surround is a bit lacking, but the price is right and the popcorn tastes better. A charmingly classic experience.

COTTAGE VIEW DRIVE-IN

Phalen/Dayton's Bluff/
Woodbury

9338 E Point Douglas Rd. S
Cottage Grove, MN 55016
(651) 458-5965 | www.manntheatersmn.com

They don't make 'em like they used to but you can still enjoy a night out at the movies at the Cottage View. Bring the lawn chairs or just crack the window and curl up in the front seat (or even the roof) and enjoy some popcorn under the stars.

DRAGON FESTIVAL

Phalen/Dayton's Bluff/
Woodbury

www.dragonfestival.org

The annual July festival in and around Lake Phalen attracts a crowd to its Pan-Asian experience that features performing acts, food and activities in the park. The main attractions are the frighteningly long dragon boats that take to the water and race for the crown.

41

LOOKOUT RIDGE

Phalen/Dayton's Bluff/
Woodbury

8595 Central Park Pl.
Woodbury, MN 55125
(651) 735-7645 | www.woodburylookoutridge.com

When the weather outside is frightful, you can still enjoy a day playing by the river in this St. Croix-themed indoor playground. Tree houses, slides, cliffs and realistic sound effects can almost make you feel like you're outdoors. There's even a cave to explore.

MOUNDS THEATER

Phalen/Dayton's Bluff/
Woodbury

1029 Hudson Rd.
St. Paul, MN 55106
(651) 772-2253 | www.moundstheater.org

The 1922 venue is full of history and provides movies and other performances throughout the year. Tours of the building focus on its supposedly haunted past and can create a spooky adventure any time of year.

VERTICAL ENDEAVORS

Phalen/Dayton's Bluff/
Woodbury

855 Phalen Blvd.
St. Paul, MN 55106
(651) 776-1430 | www.verticalendeavors.com

For a challenging adventure, try scaling the 36-foot walls of this indoor climbing facility. The artificial rock is realistic in look and feel. Instructional classes and safety equipment are provided and there are even two bouldering caves to practice on before heading to Taylors Falls for the real deal.

CINCO DE MAYO

West Side/South St. Paul/
Inver Grove Heights/
Eagan/Mendota Heights

www.districtdelsol.com

Experience the ultimate fiesta at the annual District del Sol Cinco de Mayo celebration. Filled with low-rider hydraulics, colorful parades multiple stages of authentic entertainment, the festival provides an exciting and beginning to the outdoor festival season. Pick up a piñata and bring the party home.

JONATHON PADELFORD

West Side/South St. Paul/
Inver Grove Heights/
Eagan/Mendota Heights

100 Yacht Club Rd.
St. Paul, MN 55107
www.showboat.umn.edu

Stand on the stern and watch the giant paddlewheel churn through the waters of the Mississippi as you cruise the river and enjoy the scenery. Tours depart daily during the warm season and there are plenty of hot dogs served on board.

THE BLAST

West Side/South St. Paul/
Inver Grove Heights/
Eagan/Mendota Heights

1501 Central Pkwy.
Eagan, MN 55121
(651) 675-5550 | www.ci.eagan.mn.us

Blast off in the cosmic rocket ships of this indoor playground then slide back to earth on one of the many slides. It's a great way to beat the winter chill or wait out the rain in the summer.

THE GROVE

West Side/South St. Paul/
Inver Grove Heights/
Eagan/Mendota Heights

8055 Barbara Ave.
Inver Grove Heights, MN 55077
(651) 450-2480 | www.ci.inver-grove-heights.mn.us

Splash the day away at the indoor aquatic center or get a workout in with your buddy at the fitness center. From treadmills to mushroom waterfalls, there's plenty for both of you to enjoy.

WABASHA STREET CAVES

West Side/South St. Paul/
Inver Grove Heights/
Eagan/Mendota Heights

215 Wabasha St. S
St. Paul, MN 55107
(651) 224-1191 | www.wabashastreetcaves.com

Explore the speak – easy hide – outs of notorious gangsters from the days of Prohibition. Tours of the limestone caverns that have also housed breweries and grown mushrooms can be had throughout the year. The caves also feature special events, performances and themed tours.

NICKELODEON UNIVERSE

Bloomington/Eden Prairie/
Richfield/Edina

5000 Center Ct.
Bloomington, MN 55425
(952) 883-8500 | www.nikelodeonuniverse.com

It's the grand champion of indoor amusement parks, and not because it's the only indoor amusement park around. Despite being confined under a roof, the monstrosity of roller coasters, rides and games seems to grow with every visit. An adult-friendly kid zone.

THE WORKS

Bloomington/Eden Prairie/
Richfield/Edina

5701 Normandale Rd.
Minneapolis, MN 55424
(952) 848-4848 | www.theworks.org

Designed for young engineers that like to play with their minds as well as their hands, this museum features drop-in and scheduled programs that will spark creativity and provide plenty of action. Design a mini-catapult here and you can attack the castle with confidence at home.

43

WATER PARK OF AMERICA

Bloomington/Eden Prairie/
Richfield/Edina

1700 American Blvd. E
Bloomington, MN 55425
(952) 698-8888 | www.waterparkofamerica.com

The nearby Mall of America amusement park is impressive. But it's dry. This enormous indoor water park follows the "bigger is better" theme of the area and doesn't disappoint in size, scope or volume of water and toys. Open year–round.

WAY COOL COOKING SCHOOL

Bloomington/Eden Prairie/
Richfield/Edina

16544 W 78th St.
Eden Prairie, MN 55346
(952) 949-6799 | www.waycoolcookingschool.com

Tired of macaroni and cheese in a box and frozen pizza? Attend a monthly free cooking class or sign up for an ongoing program at this creative kitchen. Designed for kids, the program gets little hands dirty mixing up ingredients and learning kitchen basics. You could probably use a few pointers yourself.

UNDERWATER ADVENTURES

Bloomington/Eden Prairie/
Richfield/Edina

120 E Broadway
Bloomington, MN 55425
(952) 883-0202 | www.underwaterworld.com

Pet the sting rays in the hands-on pool and watch the sharks swim over-head in the underwater tunnel where you're surrounded by a living coral reef environment. Educational programs and activities add to the experience.

NATIONAL SPORTS CENTER

Roseville/White Bear Lake/
Woodbury/Blaine

1700 105th Ave. NE
Blaine, MN 55449
(763) 785-5600 | www.ncscsports.com

There's always something interesting happening at the National Sports Center, whether it's pro soccer games or broomball tournaments. The 600-acre facility offers programs in over a dozen sports and you can often take in multiple sporting events on the same visit.

SUN RAY LANES

Roseville/White Bear Lake/ Woodbury/Blaine

1700 105th Ave. NE
Blaine, MN 55449
(651) 735-3222 | www.sunraylanes.com

Strike up a good time at the lanes, or at least laugh at a few gutter balls. Use the rails or play straight, knocking things down with a big, heavy ball is always a good time.

TALLY'S DOCKSIDE

Roseville/White Bear Lake/ Woodbury/Blaine

4440 Lake Ave. S
White Bear Lake, MN 55110
(651) 429-2633 | www.cghooks.com
May-September

Pack up the cooler, poles and swimming gear and get out on the lake. Pontoons and fishing boats are available to get out on the open expanse of White Bear Lake. The fishing is always good and jumping into a Minnesota lake is a right of passage.

THE LITTLE GYM

Roseville/White Bear Lake/ Woodbury/Blaine

12138 Business Park Blvd.
Champlin, MN 55316
(763) 421-5777 | www.thelittlegym.com

How many somersaults and back flips can you do? Find out at The Little Gym with a full range of programs and tumbling classes for kids of all ages. Parents are encouraged to join their kids on the mats and join in the fun.

VALL-HI DRIVE-IN

Roseville/White Bear Lake/ Woodbury/Blaine

11260 Hudson Blvd. N
Lake Elmo, MN 55042
(651) 436-7464 | www.valihi.com

It's a neighborhood icon amid the country fields. Drive-ins are a rare breed these days, so take advantage of a classic experience while you can. Get there early and fire up the grill for a personal picnic experience that can't be beat.

BUCK HILL

Shakopee/Apple Valley/ Burnsville/Lakeville

15400 Buck Hill Rd.
Burnsville, MN 55306
(952) 435-7174 | www.buckhill.com

The iconic slopes along I-35 seem sad in the summertime, but the winter snows make them spring to life with snowboarders, tubers and skiers of all ages. Ride the ski lifts up, speed to the bottom and hit the chalet for some hot chocolate. Repeat with frequency.

ELKO SPEEDWAY

Shakopee/Apple Valley/
Burnsville/Lakeville

26350 France Ave.
Elko New Market, MN 55020
(952) 461-7223 | www.elkospeedway.com

Experience the roar of the engines at this NASCAR-sanctioned track as the stock cars speed around the track in their weekly battle. Motocross events, dirt bikes, snowmobiles and monster trucks occupy the track for other events.

GREAT CLIPS IMAX THEATER

Shakopee/Apple Valley/
Burnsville/Lakeville

12000 Zoo Blvd.
Apple Valley, MN 55124
(952) 431-4629 | www.imax.com

The giant screen next door to the zoo will smack you in the face with 3 – D effects and thundering digital surround sound. It's a little pricier than the standard neighborhood cinema, but it's an immersive experience that brings special movies to life.

JUMPS & DOWNS

Shakopee/Apple Valley/
Burnsville/Lakeville

1155 Shakopee Town Square
Shakopee, MN 55379
(612) 618-2304 | www.jumpsanddowns.com

If the other area attractions haven't burned off all of your child's excess energy, you can swing in to Jumps and Downs and turn them loose on the variety of inflatable bouncy houses. If they're not ready for a nap after leaving this place, you know you've given them too much cotton candy.

MINNESOTA RENAISSANCE FESTIVAL

Shakopee/Apple Valley/
Burnsville/Lakeville

www.renaissancefest.com

Huzzah! Saucy wenches and town drunkards begging in the mud may not seem like an appropriate environment for little ones, but you have to make an exception for this annual event. Jousting tournaments, archery and knife throwing, giant turkey drumsticks, and of course the King and his court, occupy the village in the woods on weekends every August-September. Behave or you'll get tossed in the stockade and publicly ridiculed.

46

MINNESOTA ZOO

Shakopee/Apple Valley/
Burnsville/Lakeville

13000 Zoo Blvd.
Apple Valley, MN 55124
(952) 431-9200 | www.mnzoo.org

Como is charming and historical; the Minnesota Zoo is sprawling and modern. Take the monorail over the large outdoor exhibits and see the herds or wander through the indoor environments that hold all your favorites. The popular snow monkeys are endless entertainment for all ages.

VALLEY FAIR

Shakopee/Apple Valley/
Burnsville/Lakeville

1 Valleyfair Dr.
Shakopee, MN 55379
(952) 445-6500 | www.valleyfair.com
Seasonal

Thrills, chills and spills are all part of the lure of Minnesota's favorite mammoth amusement park. Unique rides, shows and carnival games will keep both of you entertained and there's plenty to do for all ages. Food stands are plentiful within or bring your own and enjoy the picnic grounds.

3RD LAIR SKATE PARK

St. Louis Park/Golden Valley
Minnetonka/Maple Grove

850 Florida Ave. S
Golden Valley, MN 55426
(763) 797-5283 | www.3rdlair.com

Show off your shredding skills or let your child teach you some new tricks while you ride the rails and hit the pipes in this indoor skate park. BMX biking sessions and skateboard sessions run regularly and you can keep your summer skills honed even when the snow flies outside.

MAPLE MAZE

St. Louis Park/Golden Valley
Minnetonka/Maple Grove

12951 Weaver Lake Rd.
Maple Grove, MN 55369
(763) 494-6500 | www.ci.maplegrove.mn.us

Turn the tots loose in a jungle-themed maze of tunnels, slides and climbing structures at this indoor community playground. Ceiling-high tree houses and a rock–climbing wall add to the adventure.

MINNETONKA BOAT CLUB

St. Louis Park/Golden Valley
Minnetonka/Maple Grove

4850 Edgewater Dr.
Mound, MN 55364
(952) 472-1220 | www.minnetonkaboats.com
Seasonal

Go stake out a claim on the island, fish or just cruise the many bays and wide–open water of Lake Minnetonka. The area's largest lake offers recreation opportunities year round, but summer is the best time to get a Jet Ski or pontoon boat and ride the waves.

MUSEUM OF BROADCASTING

St. Louis Park/Golden Valley
Minnetonka/Maple Grove

3517 Raleigh Ave.
St. Louis Park, MN 55416
(952) 926-8198 | www.museumofbroadcasting.org

Explore the days of black–and–white television (yes, they used to make those) and pre-television technology at this interesting museum. Make a recording of you and your tyke doing a radio show for a keepsake memento.

SHOWPLACE ICON

St. Louis Park/Golden Valley
Minnetonka/Maple Grove

1625 W End Blvd.
St Louis Park, Minnesota 55416
(612) 568-0375 | www.kerasotes.com

Your child will feel like a king in the luxuriously large reclining seats and personal tables. Catch all the latest releases in style at the Showplace ICON. Table-side service brings the goodies to you and you can even grab some grill-style chow while you enjoy the show.

THE BEST DAD/CHILD
STORES

BIG BRAIN COMICS   Downtown

1027 Washington Ave. S
Minneapolis, MN 55415
(612) 338-4390 | www.bigbraincomics.com

A cornucopia of comic books piled high with an extremely knowledgeable staff to help you wade through it all.

GREEN GOOBER   Downtown

5411 Nicollet Ave.
Minneapolis, MN 55419
(612) 823-2222 | www.thegreengoober.com

The Green Goober stocks an eclectic mix of eco-friendly toys, books and games. Unique gifts for green lifestyles.

JELLYCAT   Downtown

127 3rd Ave. N # 310
Minneapolis, MN 55401
(612) 332-3088 | www.jellycat.com

Hip and humorous plush toys for the sophisticated stuffed animal lover.

MACY'S   Downtown

700 On The Mall
Minneapolis, MN 55402
(612) 375-2200 | www.macys.com

A good stop anytime, the classic location is a must during the holidays for their annual winter wonderland display.

MAGERS & QUINN   Downtown

608 2nd Ave. S
Minneapolis, MN 55402
(612) 371-2002 | www.magersandquinn.com

Visit this large independent store that lends itself to hours of browsing the rows and rows of new and used books.

MANHATTAN TOY   Downtown

430 1st Ave N # 500
Minneapolis, MN 55401
(612) 337-9600 | www.manhattantoy.com

High-end toys designed for creative imaginations made with premium craftsmanship.

MIDWEST MOUNTAINEERING
Downtown

309 Cedar Ave. S
Minneapolis, MN 55454
(612) 339-3433 | www.midwestmtn.com

If you want to take a great outdoors adventure with your child, this is the place to get all the gear.

SHINDERS
Downtown

733 Hennepin Ave.
Minneapolis, MN 55402
(612) 333-3628

The local bookseller also stocks comics, magazines, sports cards and games. Multiple locations.

MAGUS BOOKS & HERBS
Minneapolis/
Northeast/Near North

1309 1/2 4th St. SE
Minneapolis, MN 55414
(612) 379-7669 | www.magusbooks.com

Take a trip to the other side at this emporium that focuses on the paranormal and metaphysical.

PACIFIER
Minneapolis/
Northeast/Near North

310 E Hennepin Ave.
Minneapolis, MN 55414
(612) 623-8123 | www.pacifieronline.com

If you've got needs for newborn wares, this urban baby boutique has the goods in a fun space just over the river from downtown.

DREAMHAVEN BOOKS
Powderhorn/Phillips
Minnehah/Nokomis

2301 E 38th St.
Minneapolis, MN 55406
(612) 823-6161 | www.pacifieronline.com

You can scratch your science fiction and fantasy itch at this popular specialty spot.

INGEBRETSEN'S
Powderhorn/Phillips
Minnehah/Nokomis

SCANDINAVIAN GIFTS & FOODS

1601 East Lake St.
Minneapolis, MN 55407
(612) 729-9333 | www.ingebretsens.com

All things Scandinavian can be found in this diverse shop that's right up Minnesota's alley. Get some unique gifts and pick up some great sausage, too.

53

MERCADO CENTRAL

Powderhorn/Phillips
Minnehah/Nokomis

1515 E Lake St # 5
Minneapolis, MN 55407
(612) 728-5401 | www.mercadocentral.net

Take a cultural trip to Latin America without leaving the city. Authentic market sells groceries and creative crafts and goods. A restaurant is on premise as well.

ORANGE RHINO KIDS

Powderhorn/Phillips
Minnehah/Nokomis

4913 28th Ave. S
Minneapolis, MN 55417
(612) 868-4914 | www.orangerhinokids.com

Your child will be the hip kid on the block when sporting the organic duds from this shop.

ST. MANE SPORTING GOODS

Powderhorn/Phillips
Minnehah/Nokomis

4159 28th Ave. S
Minneapolis, MN 55406
(612) 722-1447 | www.stmanes.com

The long – time neighborhood sporting goods store has a little bit of everything to help you get active in a wide variety of sports.

THE TWISTED GROOVE

Powderhorn/Phillips
Minnehah/Nokomis

4503 34th Ave. S
Minneapolis, MN 55406
(612) 721-3524 | www.twistedgroove.com

Take a long strange trip to The Twisted Groove for one-of-a-kind hand-dyed tie dye apparel in all sizes.

TWIN TOWN GUITARS

Powderhorn/Phillips
Minnehah/Nokomis

3400 S Lyndale Ave.
Minneapolis, MN 55408
(612) 822-3334 | www.twintown.com

Give the gift of music and let your child discover their inner rock star at Twin Town. Find music lessons and all the necessary gear in one place.

UNCLE EDGAR'S MYSTERY BOOKSTORE

Powderhorn/Phillips
Minnehah/Nokomis

2864 Chicago Ave.
Minneapolis, MN 55407
(612) 824-9984 | www.unclehugo.com

This is where super sleuths and mystery buffs go to search for their whodunits.

BEAD MONKEY

Uptown/Lakes/Lyn–Lakes/
Lowery Hill/Linden Hills

3717 W 50th St.
Minneapolis, MN 55410
(952) 929-4032 | www.thebeadmonkey.com

What's more fun than a barrel full of beads? Bead Monkey can teach your child how to make crafty creations and supply all the materials needed at two locations.

BIRCHBARK BOOKS

Uptown/Lakes/Lyn–Lakes/
Lowery Hill/Linden Hills

2115 W 21st St.
Minneapolis, MN 55405
(612) 374-4023 | www.birchbarkbooks.com

You can find hand–picked titles and hand-crafted arts and crafts at this Native American–inspired literary niche.

DOUBLE DANGER BOOKS

Uptown/Lakes/Lyn–Lakes/
Lowery Hill/Linden Hills

818 W Lake St.
Minneapolis, MN 55408
(612) 824-1692 | www.doubledangercomics.com

Toys and novelties as well as comics, books and t-shirts are available at this safe–haven for fun-seekers. They also carry a wide variety of collectibles.

KIDDYWAMPUS

Uptown/Lakes/Lyn–Lakes/
Lowery Hill/Linden Hills

4400 Excelsior Blvd.
St. Louis Park, MN 55416
(952) 926-7871 | www.kiddywampus.com

The young ones can take the toys for a test drive in the playroom or you can help them create their own. Kiddywampus carries an inspiring array of imaginative items.

MAGERS & QUINN

Uptown/Lakes/Lyn–Lakes/
Lowery Hill/Linden Hills

www.magersandquinn.com

Peruse, browse and meander the shelves to find the perfect book. New and used titles offer something for everybody.

WILD RUMPUS

Uptown/Lakes/Lyn–Lakes/
Lowery Hill/Linden Hills

2720 W 43rd St. # 1
Minneapolis, MN 55410
(612) 920-5005 | www.wildrumpusbooks.com

Stop in for story time and load up on bedtime material. Your child will love the magical atmosphere that comes complete with wandering cats, chickens and other critters that roam freely around the store. A must – visit shop for all ages.

WONDERMENT

Uptown/Lakes/Lyn–Lakes/
Lowery Hill/Linden Hills

4306 Upton Ave. S # C
Minneapolis, MN 55410
(612) 929-2707 | www.wondermentshop.com

Find something that's sure to cause an awed admiration even from the most finicky child. Imaginative natural toys, science kits, circus activities and more can be found in this mom-owned shop. Craft classes are also available.

AX-MAN

Como/Midway/Frogtown

1639 University Ave. W
St. Paul, MN 55104
(651) 646-8653 | www.ax-man.com

This amusing institution could put out a bucket of pocket lint and create a hundred imaginative uses for it. And probably has. Don't be surprised if your child screams for a nickel to buy a handful of fluffy ant pillows if they have some. Only an in-person visit can adequately describe the amazing urban rabbit – hole adventure that is Ax-Man.

MICAWBER'S BOOKS

Como/Midway/Frogtown

2238 Carter Ave.
St. Paul, MN 55108
(651) 646-5506 | www.micawbers.com

The store is small and cozy but the selection is vast. Kids will love the comfortable children's area and well-designed décor.

MIDWAY BOOKS

Como/Midway/Frogtown

1579 University Ave. W
St. Paul, MN 55104
(651) 644-7605 | www.midwaybook.com

Books, books, and more books occupy this favorite location that carries a boggling mix of well-read titles and collectible comics.

PEAPOD'S

Como/Midway/Frogtown

251 Snelling Ave. S
St. Paul, MN 55105
(651) 695-5559 | www.peapods.com

Batteries are not required at this all-natural toy and gift shop. Wood and natural fibers make up the eco-friendly selection of baby items and children's gifts you won't find anywhere else.

SOURCE COMIC & BOOKS

Como/Midway/Frogtown

1601 Larpenteur Ave. W
St. Paul, MN 55113
(651) 645-0386 | www.sourcecomicsandgames.com

Source is your source for all of your comic needs as well as anime specialties. Fight the doldrums with a selection from their huge game stock featuring hard-to-find board games and role–playing games.

BABY GRAND

Highland/Groveland-Macalister/
Summit Hill

1137 Grand Ave.
St. Paul, MN 55105
(651) 224-4414 | www.babyongrand.com

You can find chic styling for all things baby at two locations in the metro area. From furniture and toys to clothing and gear, there are even gifts for Mom.

BEAD MONKEY

Highland/Groveland-Macalister/
Summit Hill

867 Grand Ave. # 3
St. Paul, MN 55105
(651) 222-7729 | www.thebeadmonkey.com

What's more fun than a barrel full of beads? Bead Monkey can teach your child how to make crafty creations and supply all the materials needed at two locations.

CHOO CHOO BOB'S

Highland/Groveland-Macalister/
Summit Hill

2050 Marshall Ave.
St. Paul, MN 55104
(651) 646-5252 | www.choochoobobs.com

Put on your engineer's cap and play with the four tables of trains. Just watching the working displays are entertainment enough, but there's plenty of supplies available to build your own railroad empire at home.

57

COMMON GOOD BOOKS
Highland/Groveland-Macalister/
Summit Hill

165 Western Ave. N
St. Paul, MN 55102
(651) 225-8989 | www.commongoodbooks.com

Discover local literary gems and general interest titles at this intelligent and cozy shop on Cathedral Hill.

CREATIVE KIDSTUFF
Highland/Groveland-Macalister/
Summit Hill

1074 Grand Ave.
St. Paul, MN 55105
(651) 222-2472 | www.creativekidstuff.com

Challenge your child's mind with the award-winning educational and creative toys at Creative Kidstuff. The unique playthings with a purpose will help stimulate the brain cells and make their imagination spin.

RED BALLOON BOOK STORE
Highland/Groveland-Macalister/
Summit Hill

891 Grand Ave.
St. Paul, MN 55105
(651) 224-8320 | www.redballoonbookshop.com

Creative and colorful, your child will feel right at home in this magical book shop and educational toy store. Their story time shouldn't be missed and there are comfortable places to curl up with the young one for a read.

SCALE MODEL SUPPLIES
Highland/Groveland-Macalister/
Summit Hill

458 Lexington Pkwy. N
St. Paul, MN 55104
(651) 646-7781 | www.scalemodelsupplies.com

From rockets and ships, to dollhouses and coin collecting, you can find everything you need to begin a hobby or create a special project. Planes, trains, automobiles and more.

UNCLE SVEN'S COMIC SHOPPE

Highland/Groveland-Macalister/
Summit Hill

1838 Saint Clair Ave.
St. Paul, MN 55105
(651) 699-3409

Visit this nostalgic neighborhood shop that oozes character to find a complete line of comics and games that will entertain and amuse.

COLOR ME MINE

Phalen/Dayton's Bluff/
Woodbury

1551 Larpenteur Ave.
St. Paul, MN 55113
(651) 644-1726 | www.stpaul.colormemine.com

Find the perfect piggy bank, picture frame, or other special item, then sit down and hand-paint your very own one-of-a-kind creation. Shop and share the afternoon away and walk away with a treasure at three metro locations.

THE RED GIRAFFE

Phalen/Dayton's Bluff/
Woodbury

10150 City Walk Dr.
Woodbury, MN 55129
(651) 714-5427 | www.theredgiraffe.com

A baby boutique that features a wide variety of toys, clothes and all the necessary gear to start a baby out in style.

COLOR ME MINE

West Side/South St. Paul/
Inver Grove Heights/
Eagan/Mendota Heights

3324 Promenade Ave. #100
Eagan, MN 55121
(651) 454-4099 | www.eagan.colormemine.com

Find the perfect piggy bank, picture frame, or other special item, then sit down and hand-paint your very own one-of-a-kind creation. Shop and share the afternoon away and walk away with a treasure at three metro locations.

ENCHANTED TREE HOUSE

West Side/South St. Paul/
Inver Grove Heights/
Eagan/Mendota Heights

4766 Banning Ave.
White Bear Lake, MN 55110
(651) 426-7551 | www.enchantedtreehouse.com

When you want something special, this downtown White Bear Lake boutique can supply you with unique keepsake mementos, gifts, special occasion clothing, personalized blankets, and more.

MINDS EYE COMICS

West Side/South St. Paul/
Inver Grove Heights/
Eagan/Mendota Heights

1565 Cliff Rd.
Mendota Heights, MN 55122
(651) 683-0085 | www.mindseyecomics.com

The friendly staff knows their stuff when it comes to comics and collecting. They can help you and your child learn the ropes or keep you up with the latest releases.

A WORLD OF FISH

Bloomington/Eden Prairie/
Richfield/Edina

1516 E 66th St.
Richfield, MN 55423
(612) 866-2026 | www.worldoffish.com

Enjoy thousands of gallons of reef creatures, fish, and marine animals on display throughout the store and create an exotic and entertaining tank of your own.

BANANAS FOR KIDS

Bloomington/Eden Prairie/
Richfield/Edina

1157 Wayzata Blvd.
Wayzata, MN 55391
(952) 473-3383 | www.bananasforkids.com

Slip on some fun with a cool collection of clothes and novelty items for the younger set.

BUILD-A-BEAR WORKSHOP

Bloomington/Eden Prairie/
Richfield/Edina

172 E. Broadway
Bloomington, MN 55425
(952) 854-1164 | www.buildabear.com

Create your own cuddly buddy with your child at this interactive stuffed animal shop. They'll hold it closer at night knowing you helped.

CREATIVE KIDSTUFF

Bloomington/Eden Prairie/
Richfield/Edina

3555 Galleria
Edina, MN 55435
(952) 926-4512 | www.creativekidstuff.com

Challenge your child's mind with the award-winning educational and creative toys at Creative Kidstuff. The unique playthings with a purpose will help stimulate the brain cells and make their imagination spin.

HOT COMICS & COLLECTIBLES

Bloomington/Eden Prairie/
Richfield/Edina

6609 Nicollet Ave. S
Richfield, MN 55423
(612) 798-3936 | www.hotcomicsandcollectibles.com

They've got all your childhood favorites as well as the latest and greatest. Explore the well-organized collection of comics as well as a large selection of collectibles and games at two locations.

HUB HOBBY CENTER

Bloomington/Eden Prairie/
Richfield/Edina

6410 Penn Ave. S
Richfield, MN 55423
(612) 866-9575 | www.hubhobby.com

Hub Hobby Center is the hub for all of your fun – time supplies. Their hobby spokes include a large variety of remote – controlled items as well as rockets, trains, race cars, games and toys.

IKEA

Bloomington/Eden Prairie/
Richfield/Edina

8000 IKEA Way
Bloomington, MN 55425
(952) 858-8088 | www.ikea.com

It's the kid's furniture superstore that's also loaded with all manner of European-styled creations. Plus, the restaurant is one of the best deals around.

IT'S A PUZZLE

Bloomington/Eden Prairie/
Richfield/Edina

60 E Broadway
Bloomington, MN 55425
(952) 854-0314 | www.itz-a-puzzle.com

Puzzles train the brain and this shop has all the mind candy you can handle in a variety of flavors and fun.

STORES

LEGO IMAGINATION CENTER

Bloomington/Eden Prairie/
Richfield/Edina

164 Bloomington Ave. S
Bloomington, MN 55425
(952) 858-8949 | www.lego.com

Build stuff you've never dreamed of with the mountains of colorful blocks available at this flagship megashop.

MARBLES: THE BRAIN STORE

Bloomington/Eden Prairie/
Richfield/Edina

216 N Garden
Bloomington, MN 55425
(952) 854-5804
8251 Flying Cloud Dr. Suite 1220
Eden Prairie, MN 55344
(952) 943-0779 | www.marblesthebrainstore.com

Take your child's brain to the brainy gymnasium of Marbles and pick up some exercise equipment that will have them doing mental gymnastics and mind-bending tricks. Puzzles, games and creative toys all hand-picked to challenge and entertain.

POTTERY BARN KIDS

Bloomington/Eden Prairie/
Richfield/Edina

3150 Galleria, Space #3660
Edina, MN 55435
(952) 848-8705 | www.potterybarnkids.com

Spend a weekend redecorating your child's room but be sure to visit one of Pottery Barn Kids' showrooms to help you plan your project. They feature creative patterns and colorful accessories to help make your child's personal space a special place.

AIR TRAFFIC

Roseville/White Bear Lake/
Shoreview/Blaine

155 Rosedale Center #337
Roseville, MN 55113
(651) 631-3150 | www.airtrafficonline.com

Find a complete line of creative kites and hit the skies, or pick up some juggling supplies and throw some stuff in the air. The imaginative games and hobby supply store has two locations.

DOOZIE

Roseville/White Bear Lake/
Shoreview/Blaine

402 Main St.
Stillwater, MN 55082
(651) 430-3201 | www.doozieboutique.com

A chic boutique in a historic downtown, Doozie stocks clothing, toys and gifts for kids that Moms will adore and there are plenty of items for her as well.

EXOTICS & AQUATICS

Roseville/White Bear Lake/
Shoreview/Blaine

1625 County Hwy. 10 NE Suite D
Spring Lake Park, MN 55432
(763) 572-1337 | www.exo-aqua-store.com

You'll find plenty of fish supplies, but the real stars here are the lizards, snakes and furry little critters in the large display cases.

HOT SPOT SKATE SHOP

Roseville/White Bear Lake/
Shoreview/Blaine

10563 University Ave. NE
Blaine, MN 55434
(763) 754-3848 | www.hotspotskateshop.com

Get all your boarding needs, equipment and supplies at Hot Spot. Whether your child wants to shred some rails on land or hit the snowy slopes, this shop has you covered.

HUB HOBBY CENTER

Roseville/White Bear Lake/
Shoreview/Blaine

82 Minnesota Ave.
Little Canada, MN 55117
(651) 490-1675 | www.hubhobby.com

Hub Hobby Center is the hub for all of your fun–time supplies. Their hobby spokes include a large variety of remote–controlled items as well as rockets, trains, race cars, games and toys.

63

LAKESHORE LEARNING

Roseville/White Bear Lake/
Shoreview/Blaine

1721 Beam Ave.
Maplewood, MN 55109
(651) 777-0650 | www.lakeshorelearning.com

Learning has never been so fun! Pick up everything you need for school as well as create an educational experience at home. Two metro area locations.

RED RIVER KIDS

Roseville/White Bear Lake/
Shoreview/Blaine

421 Main St. S
Stillwater, MN 55082
(651) 351-7711 | www.redroverkids.com

The toys, clothes and gifts at this Main St. specialty shop are creative and colorful and designed to be childish and immature. Stop in to see why they're so popular with kids.

TOMODACHI

Roseville/White Bear Lake/
Shoreview/Blaine

156 Rosedale Center #655
Roseville, MN 55113
(651) 631-1777 | www.tomodachi.us

This shop features a knowledgeable staff and carries a happy selection of Japanese anime items and collectibles including plush toys, miniatures and art.

ABC TOY STORE

Shakopee/Apple Valley/
Burnsville/Lakeville

14003 Grand Ave.
Burnsville, MN 55337
(952) 892-7666 | www.abctoyzone.com

ABC is an elementary choice for school supplies and items to help out with science fair projects.

AIR TRAFFIC

Shakopee/Apple Valley/
Burnsville/Lakeville

2025 Burnsville Center
Burnsville, MN 55306
(952) 435-2868 | www.airtrafficonline.com

Find a complete line of creative kites and hit the skies, or pick up some juggling supplies and throw some stuff in the air. The imaginative games and hobby supply store has two locations.

EAGLE MAGIC & JOKE SHOP

Shakopee/Apple Valley/
Burnsville/Lakeville

11995 County Rd. 11
Burnsville, MN 55337
(952) 426-1716 | www.eaglemagicstore.com

Visit the oldest magic store in the country for a fun shopping experience that can yield pranks, jokes, magic tricks and even a rubber chicken.

HALF PRICE BOOKS

Shakopee/Apple Valley/
Burnsville/Lakeville

7600 150th St. W
Apple Valley, MN 55124
(952) 431-0749 | www.halfpricebooks.com

Find a large selection of new and used books as well as music and other items at great prices.

MANIC CERAMICS

Shakopee/Apple Valley/
Burnsville/Lakeville

17685 Kenwood Trail
Lakeville, MN 55044
(952) 898-6978 | www.maniceramicmn.com

Manic Ceramics has created an inviting and cozy space that will help unleash your child's creative juices. Pick from a wide selection of pottery items and help your child create a hand-painted masterpiece in their colorful studio. Create gifts for each other and trade when you're finished.

LEAPING LIZARDS

Shakopee/Apple Valley/
Burnsville/Lakeville

12601 Chowen Ave. S
Burnsville, MN 55337
(952) 894-2305 | www.leapinglizardsreptileshop.com

They've got all the cool pets that big sisters dread. Find a wide selection of snakes, spiders, frogs and lizards at this specialty reptile shop.

ZOMBIE BOARD SHOP

St. Louis Park/Golden Valley
Minnetonka/Maple Grove

15100 Buck Hill Rd.
Burnsville, MN 55306
(952) 892-0047

Hit the Zombie Board Shop before you hit Buck Hill to ensure you've got the latest gear to hit the slopes.

65

STORES

AQUATROPICS

St. Louis Park/Golden Valley
Minnetonka/Maple Grove

3549 Douglas Dr. N
Crystal, MN 55422-2415
(763) 537-0688 | www.aquatropics.com

Get native Minnesotan panfish and game fish for your child to study in their very own bedroom tank, or pick up some Koi for the pond. The colorful showroom is full of exotic and exciting displays and stocks all the supplies you'll need for a home aquarium.

BABY GRAND

St. Louis Park/Golden Valley
Minnetonka/Maple Grove

1010 Main St.
Hopkins, MN 55343
(952) 912-1010 | www.babyongrand.com

You can find chic styling for all things baby at two locations in the metro area. From furniture and toys to clothing and gear, there are even gifts for Mom.

BUILD-A-BEAR WORKSHOP

St. Louis Park/Golden Valley
Minnetonka/Maple Grove

12567 Wayzata Blvd.
Minnetonka, MN 55305
(952) 546-2327 | www.buildabear.com

Create your own cuddly buddy with your child at this interactive stuffed animal shop. They'll hold it closer at night knowing you helped.

COLOR ME MINE

St. Louis Park/Golden Valley
Minnetonka/Maple Grove

12155 Elm Creek Blvd.
Maple Grove, MN 55369
(763) 420-0005 | www.maplegrove.colormemine.com

Find the perfect piggy bank, picture frame, or other special item, then sit down and hand-paint your very own one-of-a-kind creation. Shop and share the afternoon away and walk away with a treasure at three metro locations.

HOT COMICS & COLLECTIBLES

St. Louis Park/Golden Valley
Minnetonka/Maple Grove

3532 Winnetka Ave. N
Crystal, MN 55427
(763) 593-1223 | www.hotcomicsandcollectibles.com

They've got all your childhood favorites as well as the latest and greatest. Explore the well-organized collection of comics as well as a large selection of collectibles and games at two locations.

LAKESHORE LEARNING STORE

St. Louis Park/Golden Valley
Minnetonka/Maple Grove

5699 W 16th St.
St. Louis Park, MN 55416
(952) 541-0991 | www.lakeshorelearning.com

Learning has never been so fun! Pick up everything you need for school as well as create an educational experience at home. Two metro area locations.

POTTERY BARN KIDS

St. Louis Park/Golden Valley
Minnetonka/Maple Grove

12161 Elm Creek Blvd.
Maple Grove, MN 55369
(763) 420-7338 | www.potterybarnkids.com

Spend a weekend redecorating your child's room but be sure to visit one of Pottery Barn Kids' showrooms to help you plan your project. They feature creative patterns and colorful accessories to help make your child's personal space a special place.

UBER BABY

St. Louis Park/Golden Valley
Minnetonka/Maple Grove

6015 South Lyndale Ave.
Minneapolis, MN 55419
(612) 869-0930 | www.uberbaby.com

Fun and cheeky clothing items, gifts and special items for mom occupy this funky shop in the West End complex. Get your "I'm going to grow up and get trashed at the prom" onesie, or something a little more tasteful, here.

THE BEST DAD/CHILD
OUTDOOR PARKS & RECREATION

BOOM ISLAND
Downtown

724 Sibley St. NE
Minneapolis, MN 55413
(612) 230-6400 | www.minneapolisparks.org

Explore the lighthouse and watch the boats cruise by on the river. If you want to board the Minneapolis Queen for a riverboat excursion, this is the place. Playground equipment, picnic shelters and remnants of the river's logging history provide ample activities.

ELLIOT PARK
Downtown

1000 14th St. E
Minneapolis, MN 55404
(612) 370-4772 | www.minneapolisparks.org

Cool off in the wading pool after working up a sweat on the array of playground equipment. There's plenty of green space and grassy knolls to play. The adjacent recreation center offers frequent programs for basketball, tennis, flag football and softball. Bring the skateboards for some ollies at the skate park.

LORING PARK
Downtown

1382 Willow St.
Minneapolis, MN 55403
(612) 370-4929 | www.minneapolisparks.org

An urban oasis complete with a tot lot playground, wading pool, tennis courts, basketball and shuffleboard. Skate on the pond during the winter months or bring a blanket and enjoy free music and movies in the park on select summer nights.

MILL RUINS PARK
Downtown

103 Portland Ave. S
Minneapolis, MN 55401
(612) 313-7793 | www.minneapolisparks.org

Go on a river quest along the West Bank and explore the 19th century ruins of Minneapolis' flour milling roots. Excavated features and self-guided trails take you through a wooded wonderland with St. Anthony Falls roaring nearby.

PEAVEY PARK
Downtown

730 22nd St. E
Minneapolis, MN 55404
www.minneapolisparks.org

Two giant playground areas and a wading pool attract the tots to this 7-acre play land amidst the surrounding traffic. Bring a ball or two as baseball, basketball, soccer and tennis are all possible activities. An adjacent recreation center features a variety of youth programs. Keep a lookout for the funky mosaic art.

BOTTINEAU PARK
North/Northeast/Near North

2000 2nd St. NE
Minneapolis, MN 55418
(612) 370-4958 | www.minneapolisparks.org

A popular skate park and a wading pool are among the many attractions at Bottineau. The athletic fields are active and the playground equipment is plentiful. If the weather turns sour, head indoors to the adjacent recreation center for some active sports fun in the curved-roof gymnasium.

CREEKVIEW PARK
North/Northeast/Near North

5001 Humboldt Ave. N
Minneapolis, MN 55430
(612) 370-4965 | www.minneapolisparks.org

You child's eyes will grow wide at the sight of a 30-foot tower with twisting slides winding out from three stories high. The impressive playground area also features a climbing wall and all the other bells and whistles. You can also test your mettle at the skateboard park. Take some time to explore the banks of Shingle Creek and keep on the lookout for the plentiful small wildlife.

ST. ANTHONY PARK
North/Northeast/Near North

Jefferson St. NE and Spring St. NE
Minneapolis, MN 55413
612 230-6400 | www.minneapolisparks.org

Sled down the winter sloped of May Mountain in the winter or hit the hopscotch and foursquare courts in the summer. Basketball and tennis courts are also available. Reminiscent of a schoolyard playground, complete with the requisite play equipment, St. Anthony Park is a great anytime destination by the river in the shadow of the Minneapolis skyline.

WATER POWER PARK
North/Northeast/Near North

206 Main St. SE
Minneapolis, MN 55414
www.minneapolisparks.org

This tiny new park may lack in traditional amenities but it can still provide plenty of thrills. Get up close and personal with the St. Anthony Falls as you meander along the parks interpretive trails. Pack a lunch and perch by the rails of the overlook as you dine to the roar of the Mississippi River cascading over its first dam.

OUTDOOR PARKS

WEBBER PARK
North/Northeast/Near North

4400 Dupont Ave. N
Minneapolis, MN 55412
(612) 370-4916 | www.minneapolisparks.org

A hockey and ice rink in the winter and swimming and wading pools in the summer make this a year-round destination neighborhood park. There's plenty of biking and walking paths, playground equipment and even a gardening bed where your child can get their hands dirty. Check out a book at the Webber Library to bring home for bedtime.

LAKE HIAWATHA PARK
Powderhorn/Phillips/Minnehaha

2701 E 44th St.
Minneapolis, MN 55406
(612) 370-4930 | www.minneapolisparks.org

An eight-acre playground area that includes a climbing wall is just a drop in this 241-acre park. Explore the boulders around the lake or take a dip at the beach. There's plenty of room to roam and you might stumble upon an odd looking sculpture on the park's north side. If you do, be sure to have your child place an ear to the granite and listen for the amplified sounds of nature and the city.

LAKE NOKOMIS
Powderhorn/Phillips/Minnehaha

4955 W Lake Nokomis Pkwy.
Minneapolis, MN 55417
(612) 370-4923 | www.minneapolisparks.org

Turn your child loose on Lake Nokomis's sprawling Nevo playground and let them try to navigate the maze of nets, bridges, slides and balance bobbers. If they can find their way out, hit one of the two sand beaches to cool off and enjoy the sailboats that constantly cruise the lake. Water-craft rentals are available if you want to join them out on the water. Pond hockey and skating rule the winter months.

MINNEHAHA PARK
Powderhorn/Phillips/Minnehaha

4801 South Minnehaha Park Dr.
Minneapolis, MN 55417
(612) 230-6400 | www.minneapolisparks.org

The 53-foot waterfall in the middle of the city is the big draw but it's only a small portion of the attractions at Minnehaha. The popular garden-like greenery on the river bluffs also features winding trails along the river bottoms and amidst diverse vegetation. Playground equipment is dispersed nicely with concentrated play areas around the splashy new wading pool. Give your child's arm a workout on the scenic disc golf course. Summertime concerts and outdoor concessions can help make a day of it.

PEARL PARK
Powderhorn/Phillips/Minnehaha

414 Diamond Lake Rd. E
Minneapolis, MN 55419
(612) 370-4906 | www.minneapolisparks.org

Sports are king at Pearl as the popular park and recreation center offer programs in track, gymnastics, baseball, football and soccer. Hockey and skating rinks are open in the winter. The park features plenty of playground equipment and a refreshing wading pool to help beat the summer heat. Explore the wetlands of Diamond Lake across the street and see how many waterfowl you can spot.

POWDERHORN PARK
Powderhorn/Phillips/Minnehaha

3400 15th Ave. S
Minneapolis, MN 55407
(612) 370-4960 | www.minneapolisparks.org

There's always something going on at the 68-acre Powderhorn Park. Fish the lake from the fishing pier or splash in the wading pool. Take in one of the many community celebrations held on the grounds throughout the year including arts festivals and musical events. Athletic fields, skating rinks and sledding hills will keep you and your young one active all year.

ARMATAGE PARK
Uptown/Lakes/Lyn-Lake/
Lowry Hill/Linden Hills

2500 57th St. W
Minneapolis, MN 55410
(612) 370-4912 | www.minneapolisparks.org

An 18-foot bronze sculpture is the gateway to Armatage Park's climbing walls and brightly-colored playgrounds. Challenge you child to a skateboard showdown at the skate park or play a little one-on-one on the outdoor basketball court. A wading pool is perfect for a refreshing dip in the summer and skating and hockey rinks are open in the winter.

CEDAR LAKE
Uptown/Lakes/Lyn-Lake/
Lowry Hill/Linden Hills

Cedar Lake Parkway & Basswood Rd.
Minneapolis, MN 55416
(612) 230-6400 | www.minneapolisparks.org

Bring the poles and reel in a muskie, northern pike or bass from the shores of tree-lined Cedar Lake. The park also features three sandy beaches for swimming or sand castle building and canoes and kayaks are available for a quiet paddle. The park connects with two popular bicycle paths around the lake's waters if you prefer peddling to paddling.

OUTDOOR PARKS

LAKE CALHOUN

Uptown/Lakes/Lyn-Lake/
Lowry Hill/Linden Hills

3000 Calhoun Pkwy.
Minneapolis, MN 55408
(612) 230-6400 | www.minneapolisparks.org

The view of the Minneapolis skyline towers over the trees along Calhoun shores and the activities available at the park will make you seem miles away from the city. Windsurfers and sailors race the waves and you can bike or rollerblade for more than three miles along the shoreline. Three beaches complete with playgrounds are a sunny day treat. An archery complex on the lake's southeast corner can let you and your child experience a little target practice with the bow. Fishing docks, bicycle and watercraft rentals also provide cityscape distractions.

LAKE HARRIET

Uptown/Lakes/Lyn-Lake/
Lowry Hill/Linden Hills

43rd St. W & E Lake Harriet Pkwy.
Minneapolis, MN 55409
(612) 230-6400 | www.minneapolisparks.org

Lakeside music and movies are commonplace on the shores of Lake Harriet. Enjoy a number of special events or hit the sands of two beaches for swimming and splashing fun. Watercraft rentals are available to help you get out on the inviting water of the Chain of Lakes. One of Minneapolis' treasured resources.

LYNDALE FARMSTEAD PARK

Uptown/Lakes/Lyn-Lake/
Lowry Hill/Linden Hills

3900 Bryant Ave. S
Minneapolis, MN 55409
(612) 370-4948 | www.minneapolisparks.org

For a quiet neighborhood experience, visit Lyndale Farmstead Park and enjoy the diverse playground equipment that will keep your child swinging, spinning, sliding and climbing for hours. Located in a garden-like setting, the park is active and peaceful at the same time. Walking paths lead to the Rose Gardens and Peace Garden as well as Lake Harriet. King's Hill is a favorite sledding destination during the winter.

HARRIET ISLAND
Downtown

200 Dr. Justus Ohage Blvd.
St. Paul, MN
(651) 292-7010 | www.stpaul.gov

Sprawling wide open riverside spaces are perfect for taking in the St. Paul skyline and watching the riverboats and barges sail past. The park is home to numerous outdoor concerts and other events. The playground equipment is shaped like a paddlewheel boat mirroring the nearby excursion boats. Fish the river from the boardwalks and grab a quick snack on top the roof of the Riverboat Grill.

KELLOGG MALL
Downtown

62 Kellogg Blvd. E
St. Paul, MN 55101
(651) 632-5111 | www.stpaul.gov

Get your gaze on from high above the Mississippi at the edge of downtown St. Paul. Just steps from the Science Museum and other downtown attractions, Kellogg Mall features two large water fountains that also serve as wishing wells and spectacular views of the river valley and all of the boat traffic below.

MEARS PARK
Downtown

221 5th St. E
St. Paul, MN 55101
(651) 632-5111 | www.stpaul.gov

Mears Park is home to a number of downtown events and activities with a covered band shell and central location. The diagonal stream running through the park can be fun for splashing and floating sticks or even a paper boat and the numerous small birch trees can be a welcome retreat from the heat of the surrounding concrete.

RICE PARK
Downtown

109 4th St. W
St. Paul, MN 55102
(651) 632-5111 | www.stpaul.gov

Grab a book from the stately Central Library and a hot dog from the street vendor on a sunny day and whittle away some time by the large fountain. Rice Park is a quiet respite from the bustle of downtown and the looming Landmark Center is an eye-catching backdrop. The park is home to a skating rink in the winter.

WACOUTA COMMONS
Downtown

598 Wacouta St.
St. Paul, MN 55101

Wacouta Commons reclaimed some more blacktop to add to the bounty of area parks in 2006. Small and pleasant, the park sits on the downtown's northern fringe overlooking the historic Lowertown district and providing great views of the St. Paul skyline and Cathedral. The playground area has equipment suitable for 2-5-year olds as well as 5-12-year olds.

COMO PARK
Como/Midway/Frogtown

1199 Midway Pkwy.
St. Paul, MN 55103
(651) 632-5111 | www.stpaul.gov

The grand poobah of St. Paul parks is the ultimate urban oasis. Name an outdoor activity and it's probably possible at the area's favorite inner-city bastion. Como features multiple playgrounds, an aquatic center, athletic fields, disc golf, golf, paddleboats, canoeing and fishing. Picnic spots are everywhere and there's always the zoo, conservatory and amusement park to keep you entertained.

LEWIS PARK
Como/Midway/Frogtown

900 Marion St.
St. Paul, MN 55117
(651) 632-5111 | www.stpaul.gov

Enjoy a staggering array of modern playground equipment at this hidden gem of a neighborhood park quietly tucked away in a residential area north of the Capitol. Built on synthetic turf, the playground is a maze of climbing and crawling contraptions that you'll want a shot at as well. Try out the unique splash pad but plan on getting wet. The innovative play area features five in-ground jets and two water wiggles that are certain to produce a bevy of giggles.

MARYDALE PARK
Como/Midway/Frogtown

542 Maryland Ave. W
St. Paul, MN 55117
(651) 632-5111 | www.stpaul.gov

Often obscured by Como Lake's shadow, tiny Loeb Lake in Marydale Park is a great place to teach you child how to get a line wet. The lake is stocked every year with crappies and bluegills and the Department of Natural Resources has designated it as a children's fishing pond. Get some waxies or wiggly worms and hit the pier for some bobber action. The park also has a tot lot playground to help burn off any extra energy.

NEWELL PARK
Como/Midway/Frogtown

900 N. Fairview Ave.
St. Paul, MN 55104
(651) 632-5111 | www.stpaul.gov

One of St. Paul's original parks, Newell is a 10-acre greenery that can provide a number of sports activities or quiet pursuits. Basketball, tennis, volleyball, football and soccer are all possibilities and the playground is always ready to entertain. Stay late and roast some marshmallows in the park's fire ring to wind down after an active afternoon.

WESTERN PARK
Como/Midway/Frogtown

387 Marion St.
St. Paul, MN 55103
(651) 632-5111 | www.stpaul.gov

Spark your child's creative side with a trip to this unique outdoor sculpture park that features a 70-foot kinetic sculpture and a 17-foot high bullhorn-like piece that you can yell and scream through until you're hoarse. The piece is purposely aimed at the nearby Capitol so adults can give it a try as well. Western Park also features a fun playground area and also offers a variety of arts programs.

CROSBY FARM PARK
Highland/Groveland-Macalister/
Summit Hill

2595 Crosby Farm Rd.
St. Paul, MN 55116
(651) 632-5111 | www.stpaul.org

Crosby Lake and Upper Lake are quiet destinations suitable for a day of fishing. If the panfish don't bite, which is rare, there's always walleye and northern in the Mississippi River a few steps away. The park is a beautiful natural area that beckons you to explore the nearly seven-miles of paved trails.

HIGHLAND PARK
Highland/Groveland-Macalister/
Summit Hill

1200 Montreal Ave.
St. Paul, MN 55116
(651) 632-5111 | www.stpaul.org

The centerpiece of pride for the Highland Park area, Highland Park features an array of community events and activities. Splash the day away at the popular aquatic center or teach your child how to swing the clubs at the 18-hole golf course. Sports facilities are dotted throughout the park and the playgrounds are modern and plentiful.

HIDDEN FALLS

Highland/Groveland-Macalister/
Summit Hill

1415 Mississippi River Blvd. S
St. Paul, MN 55116
(651) 632-5111 | www.stpaul.gov

Make a treasure map and go on a play-quest in search of the Hidden Falls at this Mississippi River park. Don't forget the gorp so you can snack on the way. There's plenty of activity on the river below the Ford Dam and you can always bring the fishing poles to try your luck from shore.

HILLCREST

Highland/Groveland-Macalister/
Summit Hill

1978 Ford Pkwy.
St. Paul MN 55116
(651) 695-3706 | www.stpaul.org

A true neighborhood playground that has a little bit of everything including those nostalgic spring-mounted animals you don't see too often anymore. While those may be a blast from the past, the rest of the equipment is modern adventurous. Ball fields and tennis courts also populate the park and ice skating and sledding are popular in the winter.

HOMECROFT

Highland/Groveland-Macalister/
Summit Hill

1850 Sheridan Ave.
St. Paul, MN 55116
(651) 632-5111 | www.stpaul.gov

If a walk through Hidden Falls or Crosby Farm park didn't burn up all your child's energy, swing over to nearby Homecroft park for some playtime on their large and colorful outdoor playground. A destination in itself, the park also has ball fields, tennis courts and horseshoe pits. The adjacent recreation center has plenty of indoor fun and games as well.

BEAVER LAKE

Phalen/Dayton's Bluff/Woodbury

1050 Edgewater Blvd.
St. Paul, MN 55119
www.co.ramsey.mn.us

If the crowds are too thick at Phalen, head a few blocks east to tiny Beaver Lake. You can still get in plenty wheel-time on the paved trail around the lake that passes through wooded wetlands that attract a variety of waterfowl. Try your hand at the fishing pier and enjoy a traditional father-child chat over a couple of worm-weighted bobbers.

CARVER LAKE PARK Phalen/Dayton's Bluff/Woodbury

3175 Century Ave. S
Woodbury, MN 55125
www.ci.woodbury.mn.us

Explore the woods and high bluffs along 40-acre Carver Lake then head to the beach for an afternoon at the beach. A concession stand is open during fair weather days in the summer and the park features plenty of playground equipment for climbing, swinging and sliding. Grill out at one of the barbecue pits before hitting the archery range to practice your Robin Hood skills.

KELLER REGIONAL PARK Phalen/Dayton's Bluff/Woodbury

Highway 61 near Roselawn Ave.
Maplewood, MN 55109
(651) 770-4573 | www.stpaul.gov

Take advantage of the land of lakes at the recreation rich Keller Regional Park just up the creek from Lake Phalen. Get a canoe and paddle the waters of Spoon, Kohlman, Gervais, Round and Keller lakes. Fishing from shore is easily done from many of the lakes. Picnic areas and playgrounds surround the shorelines. There are numerous trails and archery and golf are also available adventures. Don't let the snow keep you away. Cross-country ski trails twist and turn through the park and connect with the Lake Phalen area. Rental equipment is available from the park's heated chalet.

PHALEN PARK Phalen/Dayton's Bluff/Woodbury

1615 Phalen Dr.
St. Paul, MN 55106
(651) 632-5111 | www.stpaul.gov

Monster dragon boats take center stage on Lake Phalen every July for the popular racing event at the heart of the Dragon Festival. The rest of the year, Phalen is still an active attraction. Rent a sailboat or canoe and head out on the lake. There's walleye in these waters. There's a large lakeside playground adjacent to the popular sandy beach where you can spread out some towels and enjoy the lazy days of summer. A 3.2-mile path surrounds the lake and is perfect for rollerblading, biking or walking. You can even go old-school and bust out some roller skates to travel the picturesque lakeside trail.

OUTDOOR PARKS

SWEDE HOLLOW Phalen/Dayton's Bluff/Woodbury

615 7th St. E
St. Paul, MN 55106
(651) 632-5111 | www.stpaul.gov

Enchanted is often used to describe this deep ravine on Dayton's Bluff. Once an immigrant shanty-town, the area was burned out and allowed to return to its natural state more than 50 years ago. Descending down the steep stairs can be an adventure all by itself, but you'll be rewarded with a wild wonderland and a natural playground in the heart of the city sprawl. Various critters including deer can often be seen along the banks of Phalen Creek which meanders through the park. The climb back to the top may be a bit much for young ones so be sure to save some energy for the trip back to the car.

CENTRAL PARK

Roseville/White Bear Lake/
Shoreview/Blaine

www.ci.roseville.mn.us

Centered around Bennett Lake, the 225-acre Central Park in Roseville is split into five sections and connected via scenic trails. The park features four playground areas, a fishing pier, ball fields and a nature preserve with floating boardwalks. Lake Owasso Regional Park is nearby and includes a sandy swimming beach.

LAKESIDE COMMONS

Roseville/White Bear Lake/
Shoreview/Blaine

3020 Lakes Pkwy. NE
Blaine, MN 55449
(763)785-6164 | www.blaineparks.com

The newest edition to the metro area beach parks is a big hit. With a sandy beach, modern playground, canoe and kayak rentals, and beach house with concessions, it's a perfect kid-friendly park. A whimsical splash pad is a favorite highlight that delights young and old alike.

LAKE ELMO PARK RESERVE

Roseville/White Bear Lake/
Shoreview/Blaine

1515 Keats Ave.
Lake Elmo, MN 55042
(651) 430-8370 | www.co.washington.mn.us

Young tots and older kids alike will love the gently sloping, sandy-bottomed swimming pond at Lake Elmo Park Reserve. It's perfect for young waders and more experienced swimmers. The park features two playground areas with tunnels, slides and monkey bars big enough for you to join in. A campground and RV area are available if you want to make it a local overnight.

MAPLEWOOD NATURE CENTER

Roseville/White Bear Lake/
Shoreview/Blaine

2659 E 7th St.
Maplewood, MN 55119
(651) 249-2170 | www.ci.maplewood.mn.us

Go green at this hybrid combination of an activity park, nature center and eco-exhibit. You can travel the trails in search of birds and waterfowl, visit the butterfly park or view the exhibits at the free visitor center. Composting and rainwater gardens help teach eco-friendly practices. Join in the fun of the natural playground where logs, boulders, stepping stones and bridges replace the typical plastic constructions.

SHOREVIEW COMMONS

Roseville/White Bear Lake/
Shoreview/Blaine

4650 N Victoria St.
Shoreview, MN 55126
www.shoreviewmn.gov

A quirky-looking space-age playground is a can't-miss climbing adventure at this 40-acre community park. The ziggy-zaggy and curved blue rails will generate enthusiasm at first glance. Bring the boards and ride the rails at the adjacent Sweet Roll Skate Park. Watch your child closely. They might teach you some new tricks.

LAKE MINNETONKA REGIONAL PARK

St. Louis Park/Golden Valley/
Minnetonka/Maple Grove

4610 County Rd. 44
Minnetrista, MN 55331
(763) 694-7754 | www.ci.minnetrista.mn.us

A big lake requires a big play area and the 20,000-square foot nautical-themed playground at Lake Minnetonka Regional Park does its namesake lake justice. If you don't lose your child in this behemoth of a jungle gym, slip over the lakeshore for a picnic or cool down at the sandy swimming beach.

ST. LOUIS PARK OUTDOOR AQUATIC PARK

St. Louis Park/Golden Valley/ Minnetonka/Maple Grove

3700 Monterey Dr.
St. Louis Park, MN 55416
(952) 924-2540 | www.stlouispark.org

Join in the splashing fun of this 20,000-square foot water wonderland. With two twisting, turning tube slides and plenty of geysers and splash toys, you might find your youth again while trying to keep up with your tot. A wet sand playground is perfect for creating a squishy work of art. Open weather permitting.

WEAVER LAKE COMMUNITY PARK

St. Louis Park/Golden Valley/ Minnetonka/Maple Grove

12951 Weaver Lake Rd.
Brooklyn Park, MN
(763) 494-6500 | www.ci.maple-grove.mn.us

This is a gem of a facility in the northwest metro. The park features a sandy beach with concessions and bath facilities, fishing pier, a large tube slide to the beach and two large playground areas as well as a large space net for active tots. Picnic areas and multiple sports facilities help to round out the action.

ELM CREEK PARK

St. Louis Park/Golden Valley/ Minnetonka/Maple Grove

12400 James Deane Pkwy.
Brooklyn Park, MN 55369
(763) 694-7894 | www.threeriversparks.org

At 4,900 acres, there's plenty to explore at Elm Creek Park. The swimming pond is a man-made outdoor pool surrounded by sandy beach. Concessions are available. A nature center contains live frogs, salamanders and other tiny critters for your young one to see. The outdoor nature contains a variety of wildlife viewable from the woods and wetland trails. Other activities to fill your day include canoeing, disc golf, golf, tennis, archery and oodles of playgrounds. The winter brings a full slate of cold-weather fun in the form of snowboarding, downhill and cross-country skiing, snowshoeing, sledding and tubing.

THEODORE WIRTH PARK

St. Louis Park/Golden Valley/
Minnetonka/Maple Grove

1339 Theodore Wirth Pkwy.
Minneapolis, MN 55411
(612) 230-6400 | www.minneapolisparks.org

Sample a little bit of everything at this diverse 759-acre outdoor playground. Playgrounds and picnic areas are abundant. Recreational facilities for sports are also plentiful. Natural areas include a quaking bog, fishing lakes, wildflower gardens and bird sanctuary. Trails are numerous. The park stays active in the winter with a Swiss-style chalet that is the headquarters for snowboarding areas, sledding and tubing hills as well as cross-country ski trails.

ANTLERS PARK

Shakopee/Apple Valley/
Burnsville/Lakeville

9740 201st St. W
Lakeville, MN 55044
(952) 985-4400 | www.ci.lakeville.mn.us

A favorite of locals, Antler Park features another nice beach on another nice lake. This Lake Marion hot spot features a nice playground, plenty of shade and picnic areas, and a fishing pier. A large water and sand play area for tots make this a great choice for the young ones. Take the Juno trail to the other side of the lake for some mega-play structures.

CLIFF FEN PARK

Shakopee/Apple Valley/
Burnsville/Lakeville

120 East Cliff Rd.
Burnsville, MN 55337
(952) 854-5900 | www.ci.burnsville.mn.us

The wooden Skyland Playground at Cliff Fen Park is a popular climbing and crawling attraction and more traditional playground equipment will offer a colorful alternative. The park also serves as a gateway to a 1,400-acre wildlife refuge that features white pelicans and, if you're lucky, some majestic bald eagles.

KELLEY PARK

Shakopee/Apple Valley/
Burnsville/Lakeville

6855 Fortino St.
Apple Valley, MN 55124
(952) 953-2500 | www.ci.apple-valley.mn.us

Kids love the excitement of chasing through the giant sprinklers of the splash pad. The large circular area is littered with spray nozzles and hoops to run through. A large playground area provides plenty of dry activities and picnic spots are plentiful.

MURPHY-HANREHAN PARK RESERVE

Shakopee/Apple Valley/ Burnsville/Lakeville

15501 Murphy Lake Rd.
Savage, MN 55378
(763) 694-7777 | www.threeriversparks.org

Load up your mountain bikes and head for the hilly terrain of Murphy-Hanrehan Park Reserve. The trails are a favorite spot for off-road biking. Watch out for horses. Younger children will enjoy the diverse wildlife in the park.

SANDVENTURE WATER PARK

Shakopee/Apple Valley/ Burnsville/Lakeville

1101 Adams St.
Shakopee, MN 55379
(952) 233-3840 | www.ci.shakopee.mn.us

Show your child you're not afraid to tackle the 300-foot waterslide and you might find a willing play partner all day. Then tackle the two 12-foot drop slides and diving board at this man-made, natural-looking swimming pond surrounded by sand. It's a giant chlorinated beach complete with snack shop.

CHEROKEE PARK

West Side/South St. Paul/ Inver Grove Heights/ Eagan/Mendota Heights

700 Cherokee Heights Blvd.
St. Paul, MN 55107
(651) 632-5111 | www.stpaul.org

High on the bluffs overlooking the Mississippi and St. Paul skyline, Cherokee Park offers some nice modern playground equipment and other recreational opportunities such as basketball, baseball and tennis. Picnic at the barbecue pit then head off on an adventure down the bluff trail to more parkland below. Save some time for a pre-bedtime fire at the fire pit to reflect on your day together.

FORT SNELLING STATE PARK

West Side/South St. Paul/ Inver Grove Heights/ Eagan/Mendota Heights

101 Snelling Lake Rd.
St. Paul, MN 55111
(612) 725-2389 | www.dnr.state.mn.us

An outdoor jewel in the heart of the cities, Fort Snelling State Park can be explored in a variety of ways. Visit the living museum at the 1820's historic fort to see soldiers fire muskets and cannons. Don't forget to snag some authentic rock candy from the general store. Six lakes and two rivers provide plenty of water-based recreation including a swimming beach on Lake Snelling. Paved and natural trails wind throughout the sprawling natural area with playgrounds located on Picnic Island as well as at the Lake Snelling Beach.

KAPOSIA PARK

West Side/South St. Paul/
Inver Grove Heights/
Eagan/Mendota Heights

1028 Wilde Ave. S
St. Paul, MN 55075
www.soutstpaul.org

Home to a premier 18-hole disc golf course, Kaposia Park is an easily accessible destination to get away for an afternoon. The park also has horseshoe and volleyball pits should the urge to play in the sand strike. The park connects via trail with Simon's Ravine which is an enjoyable nature area perfect for a walk-n-talk.

LILYDALE REGIONAL PARK

West Side/South St. Paul/
Inver Grove Heights/
Eagan/Mendota Heights

950 Lilydale Rd.
St. Paul, MN 55118
(651) 632-5111 | www.stpaul.org

Rumble along the river in search of ruins and rocks. Lilydale offers a natural playground in the woods that also features Pickerel Lake and the remnants of the flooded-out community that moved to the top of the bluffs. Visit the bat caves and see old kilns in the once industrious brickyards. You can even dig for 500-million year-old fossils with a permit from the parks department office.

TRAPP FARM PARK TUBING HILL

West Side/South St. Paul/
Inver Grove Heights/
Eagan/Mendota Heights

841 Wilderness Run Rd.
Eagan, MN 55123
(651) 675-5500 | www.ci.eagan.mn.us

When the snow flies, so do the tubes at this popular sliding hill in Eagan. Tubes are available for a modest fee and children under 42-inches are free. The park has a number of outdoor activity programs and hosts groups for birthday parties. When you've had your fill of the downhill bouncy-bounce, lace up some skates and hit the skating rink.

CENTENNIAL LAKES PARK

Bloomington/Eden Prairie/
Richfield/Edina

7499 France Ave. S.
Edina, MN 55435
(952) 833-9580 | www.ci.edina.mn.us

You can fish from the paddleboats or just cruise around the fountains on the 10-acre lake in the middle of a manicured setting. Try your hand at remote-controlled yachts or try to navigate the park's maze. Norwegian sleds and ice skates rule the lake in winter as the entire 10-acres are turned into a skating rink. Three bonfire areas and hot chocolate concessions will help keep you warm.

OUTDOOR PARKS

EDINBOROUGH PARK

Bloomington/Eden Prairie/
Richfield/Edina

7700 York Ave. S.
Edina, MN 55435
(952) 833-9540 | www.ci.edina.mn.us

It's a topsy-turvy world at this indoor oasis. When the weather isn't co-operating outdoors, Edina has created an outdoor park inside. Heavily landscaped with more than 6,000 trees and plants, the facility features a wonderfully whimsical playground with tree-wrapping slides, climbing nets and crawling tubes. An Olympic-sized swimming pool, running track and state-of-the-art gymnasium will tucker the tykes out in no time.

HYLAND PARK RESERVE

Bloomington/Eden Prairie/
Richfield/Edina

10145 Bush Lake Rd
Bloomington, MN 55438
(763) 694-7687 | www.ci.bloomington.mn.us

Yes, there are canoes, paddleboats, multiple lakes, snowboarding and downhill skiing, a monster sled hill, disc golf, fishing and a sprawling nature center filled with wildlife. But all of that will pale in comparison when your child gets a whiff of the gigantic creative playground that is a sprawling maze of intermingling slides, nets, climbing apparatuses and hiding nooks. Going home might be a problem.

MINNESOTA VALLEY NATIONAL WILDLIFE REFUGE

Bloomington/Eden Prairie/
Richfield/Edina

3815 American Blvd. E
Bloomington, MN 55425
(952) 854-5900 | www.fws.gov/midwest/minnesotavalley

Stop into the kid-oriented visitor center and learn about the natural treasures in the park. Pick up a nature book from the Blufftop Bookshop inside then head out on a half-mile trail through forests, prairie and wetland in search of all types of critters.

STARING LAKE PARK

Bloomington/Eden Prairie/
Richfield/Edina

13600 Pioneer Trail
Eden Prairie, MN 55347
www.edenprairie.org

The 700-foot sledding hill is a whee-fest in the winter and a warming house can keep you recharged between runs. Skating rinks and ski trails are also abundant. A hodge-podge of recreation blossoms at the park during warmer weather including archery, disc golf, fishing, boating and biking. Swings and slides? Check.

THE BEST DAD/CHILD
SPORTING EVENTS

MINNESOTA TWINS PROFESSIONAL BASEBALL

Downtown
Minneapolis

351-413 5th Ave. N
Minneapolis, MN 55401
(612) 338-9467 | www.minnesota.twins.mlb.com
April-October

Outdoor baseball is back. Target Field is a gem of a stadium and the wide-eyed thrill you're young one will receive when they first see the playing field with the Minneapolis skyline as the backdrop is a moment you'll both remember for a long time. Bring a glove and arrive early for batting practice and your best chance at snagging a souvenir.

MINNESOTA VIKINGS PROFESSIONAL FOOTBALL

Downtown
Minneapolis

900 S 5th St.
Minneapolis, MN 55415
(612) 332-0386 | www.vikings.com
September-January

Ragnar firing up the Harley is always a crowd-pleaser and the purple faithful are always trying their best to raise the roof off of Mall of America Field. Brush up on the Vikings' fight song and break it out after each score. Don't forget the purple face paint. Start 'em young and make them fans before the Cheeseheads get 'em.

MINNESOTA TIMBERWOLVES PROFESSIONAL BASKETBALL

Downtown
Minneapolis

600 N 1st Ave.
Minneapolis, MN 55403
(612) 673-1600 | www.nba.com/timberwolves
October-June

Howl at the hoopsters on the hard court at Target Center. Slam dunks, sweet shots and plenty of dribbling. What kid doesn't like bouncing balls? After the game, hit the driveway for some one-on-one.

MINNESOTA WILD PROFESSIONAL HOCKEY

Downtown
St. Paul

175 Kellogg Blvd. W
St. Paul, MN 55102
(651) 265-4800 | www.wild.nhl.com
October-April

There's always fast action on the ice at the Excel Energy Center. Snag a couple of sodas, some nachos and a pretzel and settle in for some slap-shots and hard checks off the boards. If you're lucky, you might get to ride the Zamboni in between periods.

MINNESOTA GOPHERS COLLEGE ATHLETICS

Minneapolis/Glenwood/
St. Anthony/Dinkytown

4 SE Oak St.
Minneapolis, MN 55455
(612) 624-8080 | www.gophersports.com

There are plenty of options on the University of Minnesota campus to root for the Maroon and Gold. The new TCF Bank stadium brings football back outside into the elements while basketball in The Barn is a classic experience. Mariucci Arena is filled with hockey tradition. Check with the athletic department for the full schedule of gymnastics, soccer, wrestling, swimming, track and other sports.

MINNESOTA LYNX PROFESSIONAL WOMEN'S BASKETBALL

Downtown
Minneapolis

600 N 1st Ave.
Minneapolis, MN 55403
(612) 673-1600 | www.wnba.com/lynx
April - August

The Lynx can put on a show and their brand of basketball brings plenty of excitement to downtown Minneapolis. With homegrown talent Lindsey Whalen in the fold for the foreseeable future, the Lynx have ignited a growing fan base and plenty of heroics for local youth to look up to.

ST. PAUL SAINTS MINOR LEAGUE BASEBALL

St. Paul/Como/
Midway/Frogtown

1771 Energy Park Dr.
St. Paul, MN 55108
(651) 644-6512 | www.saintsbaseball.com
May-August

Known more for their between–inning shenanigans than the names on their roster, the Saints are still a favorite, an entertaining, outdoor baseball experience in cozy Midway Stadium. Enjoy some hot dogs in a great family atmosphere and an intimate venue that will get you close to all the on–field action.

91

SPORTING EVENTS

MINNESOTA SWARM PROFESSIONAL LACROSSE

Downtown
St. Paul

175 Kellogg Blvd. W
St. Paul, MN 55102
(651) 265-4800 | www.mnswarm.com
January-April

It's played with a ball but it might not be a sport you're used to. Check out a unique sport and see how the pros play in the comfy interior of the Excel Energy Center. The fast-paced action might just light a desire for your child to pursue a different path.

MINNESOTA STING MINOR LEAGUE FOOTBALL

Downtown
St. Paul

www.stingfootball.net
April-July

Become part of "The Hive" and check out the buzz of Minor League Football played predominately in Roseville as well as other locations in the metro area. The squad plays a nine-game schedule and provides a great football fix to fill the spring and summer months.

MINNESOTA ROLLERGIRLS ROLLER DERBY

Downtown
St. Paul

2751 Hennepin Ave. S #176
Minneapolis, MN 55408
(612) 296-4743 | www.mnrollergirls.com

It might be a little raucous for the little ones, but the Minnesota Rollergirls put on a full slate of flat-track roller derby bouts at the Roy Wilkins Auditorium and advertise as being kid-friendly with a PG-13 rating. Events feature live bands and a chance for kid participation on the track.

U.S. POND HOCKEY CHAMPIONSHIPS

www.uspondhockey.com

Held in January each year, skaters from all over the country take part on 18 rinks on the frozen surface of Twin City area lakes. Played the way hockey was meant to be played – outdoors – the tournament features plenty of heated tents, activities, open skating areas and bonfires. Dates and locations may vary.

INNER CITY TENNIS
NON-PROFIT YOUTH
TENNIS PROGRAM

Uptown/Lakes/Lyn–Lakes/
Lowry hill/Linden hills

4005 Nicollet Ave.
Minneapolis, MN 55409
(612) 824-6099 | www.innercitytennis.org

This year-round complex focuses on teaching your child leadership skills and other life lessons in addition to attention–span–friendly tennis instruction. Suitable for ages 3 and up, the program boasts a marked increase in behavioral improvements of participants so your kids don't act like Johnny Mac in their everyday lives. Special events feature team play opportunities.

MINNESOTA VIXEN
WOMEN'S TACKLE FOOTBALL

www.minnesotavixen.us
April-July

Since 1999, these female gladiators have been hitting the gridiron in full pads and tearing up the turf. The Independent Women's Football League has grown to more than 40 teams and was a pioneer in female athletics. Check their website for updates on game locations, times and other events.

TWIN CITIES MARATHON

www.mtcmarathon.org

Hailed as the one of the most beautiful marathons in the nation, the Twin Cities Marathon is run each October through the streets of both cities. If you're not quite up to running the whole route, there's also 10k and 5k options as well as a host of other family activities surrounding the event. Find a good spot and plop down a lawn chair and you and your child can join in the clapping and encouragement as the runners stream by in droves.

PARKS & RECREATION
YOUTH SPORTS LEAGUES

www.minneapolisparks.org
www.stpaul.gov

Great opportunities exist to help your child meet new friends and work on their physical fitness with a variety of park and recreation programs. Check with your local recreation center for information regarding gymnastics, wrestling, rowing, golf, soccer, tennis, baseball, softball, swimming and basketball programs. League play in many sports and drop-in activities are available to test the waters of most sports.

MINNESOTA SCUBA DIVING

www.mnscuba.com

Ever wonder what lies beneath the 10,000 lakes? Scuba diving is the way to find out. There are a number of dive shops that offer year–round instruction for youth in and around the Twin Cities. Join your child in learning how to breathe underwater in the pool then head out to some of the great crystal-clear lakes that are popular with local divers. Or plan that beach getaway in the winter and go explore a coral reef in the Caribbean. Many shops offer one-day introduction classes to help you get your feet wet.

THE BEST DAD/CHILD
UNIQUE ADVENTURES

UNIQUE ADVENTURES

TAYLORS FALLS/INTERSTATE STATE PARK

www.taylorsfalls.govoffice.com
www.dnr.state.mn.us/state_parks/interstate
Within one hour

The unique volcanic pothole formations in Interstate State Park make for a dazzling natural playground for climbing and exploring the cliffs along the St. Croix River. Plenty of opportunities exist for canoeing, biking and hiking the trails on both the Minnesota and Wisconsin sides. Watch expert climbers scale the craggy cliffs or join in with a novice instructional class. There are plenty of amusement diversions as well such as a water park, mini-golf, ice cream shops and cruises of The Dalles offered by many tour boats.

GONDOLA ROMANTICA

Nelson St. in front of the Dock Cafe
425 E Nelson St.
Stillwater, MN 55082
(651) 439-1783 | www.gondolaromantica.com
May-October
Within a half – hour

Plan a special evening and let a singing gondolier guide you along the beautiful St. Croix River Valley. Packages are available that let you picnic in the boat or enjoy a meal before or after your adventure at the waterfront Dock Café. Enjoy a pre-ordered gourmet meal or pack a cooler with your own desserts and beverages. The gondolas can accommodate up to six people. Special full moon events can provide a memorable evening your child won't soon forget.

WELCH MILL CANOEING & TUBING

Welch, MN 55089
(651) 388-9857 | www.welchmillcanoeandtube.com
Open daily from Memorial Day –Labor Day.
Call for April, May and October hours.
Within an hour

It's just like the lazy river rides at the water parks, except it really is on a river. Pack a cooler with all your favorite goods and spend a relaxing day floating the Cannon River on an innertube. One-hour and four – hour trips are available and shuttle service is included in the modest rental fee. Stop and splash on the sandbars to cool off and get in a little play time along the way. Canoes and kayaks are also available.

MYSTERY CAVE/NIAGARA CAVE

Mystery Cave
21071 County Hwy. 118
Preston, MN 55965
(507) 937-3251 | www.dnr.state.mn.us/mystery_cave

Niagara Cave
P.O. Box 444 Harmony
MN 55939
(800) 837-6606 | www.niagaracave.com
Within two hours

Plan on camping at Forestville State Park in Preston and spend a couple of days spelunking underground for a memorable adventure. Both caves feature underground pools, 400–million–year old fossils and enough stalactites and stalagmites to keep your child fascinated throughout the tours. The caves are a constant 48 degrees year-round so dress warm even in summer. Mystery Cave offers a variety of tours from the standard one–hour tour to introductory wild caving tours and educational trips. Niagara Cave features a 60-foot underground waterfall and a gift shop with plenty of souvenir rocks. Bring a fishing pole and enjoy the blue–ribbon trout streams that wind past your campsite in Forestville State Park when you're not underground. Don't forget the flashlight and headlamps. Open daily Memorial Day-Labor Day. Hours vary on weekends and other days in spring and fall.

UP, UP & AWAY

Plane Rides
youngeagles.com/programs

Helicopter Rides
www.partypop.com/categories/Helicopter_Rides/Minneapolis.htm

Hot–Air Balloon Rides
www.1800skyride.com

If you're seeking some ultimate thrills, take your child on an air adventure high above the city. There are a number of services that provide airplane, helicopter and hot air balloon rides within the metro area. From small prop and twin–engine planes, to whirly-birds and quiet, lazy floats, getting a bird's–eye view is sure to rank high in childhood memories and make your child's thrill meter soar. If possible, keep an eye out for your house or other recognizable landmarks that your child can relate to that will really showcase the high-flying perspective.

HIDDEN FALLS HIKE

Nerstrand State Park
9700 170th St. E
Nerstrand, MN 55053
(507) 333-4840
www.dnr.state.mn.us/state_parks/nerstrand_big_woods/index.html
www.nerstrandmeats.com/
Within one and a half hours.

Stop at the Nerstrand Meat Market just south of Northfield and load up on some beef jerky, homemade hot dogs and other lunch treats. It's a trip back in time that serves kid-friendly samples. Then pop over to the Nerstrand State Park for a fun hike down to the scenic Hidden Falls for the perfect picnic spot. There's a lot to explore in the Big Woods and the jerky is worth the trip all by itself. Spring will provide the highest water flow with plenty of wildflowers to learn about. Fall brings eye-popping colors to the woods and is an especially popular time to visit. Hidden Falls is a special place and you can spend hours playing above the falls in the shallow creek or in the picturesque pool below. Camping is available.

SPAM MUSEUM

1101 N Main St.
Austin, MN 55912
1 (800) LUV-SPAM | www.spam.com/games/Museum
Within one and a half hours.

Scramble up some eggs with a little green food coloring and fry up a can a SPAM for breakfast to let your child know that today is going to be...a little different. Have you ever wondered what goes into this mystery meat in a can? The SPAM museum has all the answers and they're delivered inside an interactive 16,500 square-foot free museum that's designed with plenty of kid appeal. Hands-on exhibits let your child work in the factory, be a game show contestant, learn the Monty Python SPAM song and more. If you get hungry, don't worry, there's an on-site cafeteria with a menu that serves plenty SPAMified treats and goodies as well as traditional snacks.

LEBANON HILLS REGIONAL PARK

Shakopee/Apple Valley/
Burnsville/Lakeville

12100 Johnny Cake Ridge Rd.
Apple Valley, MN 55124
(952) 891-7000
www.co.dakota.mn.us – Search Lebanon Hills Regional Park

The Boundary Waters Canoe Area Wilderness is Minnesota's quintessential outdoor experience with over 1 million acres of outdoor solitude along the Canadian border. Lebanon Hills Regional Park is admittedly much smaller and more crowded (and there's no moose or bear), but it's a great urban experience that can provide good training for a trip "Up North." Canoes and kayaks are available at the park, or bring your own and paddle the five-mile water trail that traverses numerous lakes complete with Boundary Waters-type portage trails. The fishing is good and there's still plenty of wildlife to be found within this 2,000-acre metro "wilderness." A campground has modern facilities for overnight and multi-day stays. Other activities include sand castles at the swimming beach and mountain –biking the numerous off-road trails. And of course, there's also plenty of playground equipment.

BUNKER PARK STABLES

550 Bunker Lake Blvd.
Andover, MN 55304
(763) 757-9445 | www.bunkerparkstable.com
Within an hour.

Be a cowboy for a day and let your child play Hopalong Cassidy at one Bunker Park Stable just north of the metro area in Andover. Experience a variety of environments and trails suitable for young children. Eight-year olds and up can ride on their own and the stable features pony rides for the younger tots. Hour-long rides are common and provide plenty of time for your child to make a new four-footed friend. Bunker Park Stable is open year-round but hours may vary.

LARK TOYS

171 T-100
Kellogg, MN 55945
(507) 767-3387 | www.larktoys.com
Open daily March-December.
Hours vary during January and February.
Within two hours

It's like Santa's workshop all year long. Nestled in the bluffs of the scenic Mississippi River Valley, family-owned and operated LARK Toys is a treasure-trove of little-tyke nirvana in the sleepy town of Wabash, which is known more for "Grumpy Old Men" than happy kids. The monstrous retail outlet is filled with nostalgic collectibles and handmade gems. There are plenty of creative and challenging toys as well as gag items and marbles. Interactive play areas will keep your child busy and the colorful hand-carved horse carousel is a can't-miss attraction easily worth the $1 cost per ride. A waterfall–laden mini-golf course provides plenty of scenic putt-putt action with the river bluffs as a backdrop and ice cream, fudge and snack shops can provide all the energy you need to see it all.

BACKPACKING AFTON

6959 Peller Ave. S
Hastings, MN 55033
(651) 436-5391 | www.dnr.state.mn.us/state_parks/afton/
Within an hour

Strap on the packs and enjoy the great Minnesota outdoors. For an introductory backpacking adventure the 28-campsite rustic campground at Afton State Park can't be beat. Located approximately one-mile from the parking lot, the campsites can be reached by scenic trails along the bluff–tops of the Mississippi River and provide a solitary feel perfect for campfires and late–night stories. Firewood is available near each campsite and vault toilets can be an adventure on their own.

OSCEOLA & ST. CROIX VALLEY RAILWAY

114 Depot Rd.
P.O.Box 176
Osceola, WI 54020
(715) 755 3570 | www.mtmuseum.org/oscv.shtml
Open May-October on weekends, holidays and for special events.
Within an hour

Climb aboard a classic Soo Line choo-choo for a 1.5-hour scenic train journey through the St. Croix River Valley. Keep on the lookout for waterfalls and wildlife as you ride the rails along a 20-mile stretch of river. A postal car explains how mail was delivered back in the days of yore and the concession car is filled with refreshments.

FOSSIL DIGGING AT LILYDALE

Westside/South St. Paul/
Inver/Grove Heights
Eagan/Mendota

950 Lilydale Rd.
St. Paul, MN 55118
(651) 632-5111 | www.stpaul.gov/index.aspx?NID=1560

What kid doesn't like to play in the dirt? Pretend you're Louis Leakey, famous paleontologist, and seek some fossil treasure at the Brickyard in Lilydale Regional Park. 500–million–year–old trilobites, brachiopods and other pre–dinosaur paleontological prizes await your bounty bag (a Ziploc baggie with tissue paper to protect the fragile shells will do). Bring a toothbrush and garden tools to help dig out your finds. Permits are required to dig and are available through the city of St. Paul website. Bring your own refreshments and visit the bat cave, old kilns, waterfall and Pickerel Lake after your dig.

TAPESTRY FOLKDANCE CENTER

Powderhorn/Phillips/
Minnehaha

3748 Minnehaha Ave.
Minneapolis, MN 55406
(612) 722-2914 | www.tapestryfolkdance.org

Do-si-do, twirl and whirl during the monthly Family Folkdance program at Tapestry Folkdance Center. Join your child on the studio floor as live fiddlers rosin up their bows to provide the music for a variety of traditional folk dances from regions near and far. It's rare to find a dance program where the parents can join in the fun. If the stomping and clapping of the Euro-American dances don't make your child smile, the sight of you trying to keep up certainly will.

HOUSE OF BALLS

Downtown

212 3rd Ave N # 108
Minneapolis, MN 55401
(612) 332-3992 | www.houseofballs.com
Hours vary widely. Open whenever the artist is home.

If your child likes quirky, odd and completely off-the-wall, then hanging out at the front window of this shop will be a dream come true. Local artist Allen Christian has created a mysterious and delightful storefront in the Warehouse District. Control Christian's creative scrap–yard contraptions on the inside and make them reanimate by pushing the buttons outside. If the artist is home, ring the doorbell and you might be able to get a private tour of the amazing Willy Wonka-like interactive art studio.

FOSHAY TOWER OBSERVATION DECK

Downtown

821 Marquette Ave. S
Minneapolis, MN 55402
(612) 215-3700
www.nrhp.mnhs.org/property_overview.cfm?propertyID=27
Open daily. Subject to closing during weather conditions.

It once commanded the Minneapolis skyline and while it has since been dwarfed by the IDS and other modern skyscrapers, the Foshay Tower can still boast the only public observation deck in town. And the view is pretty spectacular. Your child will thrill at the 31st–floor panoramic view that stretches for miles. Get up close and personal with the IDS Center's mid-section and see if you can spot yourself in the reflections off its modern mirrored sides.

MOSAIC ON A STICK
Como/Midway/Frogtown

595 Snelling Ave. N
St. Paul, MN 55104
(651) 645-6600 | www.mosaiconastick.com
Closed Sundays and Mondays.

Not only do you get to break stuff at the cheekily named Mosaic on a Stick near the State Fairgrounds, but you get to piece the stuff you break back together in puzzle fashion to create a keepsake treasure. The art studio has all the supplies and helpful instruction you need to create an original work of mosaic art limited only by your child's imagination. The next time your child accidentally breaks a plate, pick up the pieces and turn it into a fun, adventurous experience. Or you can just drop in and use the tiles available at the store. Make a picture frame for your child's dresser and fill it with a photo from a different unique adventure.

FROM THE AUTHOR

I hope that dads can find plenty of ideas in this book to help them be heroes to their kids—not just on special days or days when they explore some of the places and events in this book together—but every day. Opportunities to create memories present themselves wherever you look.

The Twin Cities area is blessed with a bounty of resources that enrich a child's life and strengthen their family relationships. We need only take action to be able to enjoy them. So put on your cape and let your daddy powers loose. May the memories you make last a lifetime.

Thank you to Brooklyn, Kaden, Cody and Cole for being the inspiration for this book. We have a lot of things to see and do ahead of us. And thank you to Shelley for being such a WonderMom. A special thanks to all my friends and family for their help with everything.

Yours, Troy Thompson

ABOUT THE AUTHOR

Troy Thompson is a professional journalist, author, freelance writer and native Twin City resident. He has written for a variety of national parenting resource publications as a contributing blogger and features writer and also covers metro area news events for local publications. Thompson has also written extensively on Minnesota's outdoors, recreational opportunities, restaurants and entertainment offerings for numerous national outlets. He is a father of four active children, ages six to twelve, who are his reason for writing this guide.